barefoot contessa
foolproof

ina garten

barefoot contessa
foolproof

recipes you can trust

PHOTOGRAPHS BY QUENTIN BACON

Clarkson Potter/Publishers *New York*

Photographs on pages 88-89, 162-163, 214-215, and
256-257 copyright © 2012 by John Hall

Published in the United States by
Clarkson Potter/Publishers, an imprint of the
Crown Publishing Group, a division of
Random House, Inc., New York.
www.crownpublishing.com
www.clarksonpotter.com

CLARKSON POTTER is a trademark and
POTTER with colophon is a registered
trademark of Random House, Inc.

Library of Congress Cataloging-in-Publication Data
Garten, Ina.
Barefoot Contessa foolproof / Ina Garten. — 1st ed.
Includes index.
1. Cooking.   I. Title.
TX714.G36425   2012
641.3—dc23   2012007526

ISBN 978-0-307-46487-3
eISBN 978-0-7704-3340-6

Printed in Hong Kong

Design by Marysarah Quinn
All photographs with the exception of those noted
above are by Quentin Bacon.
10 9 8 7 6 5
First Edition

For Jeffrey, he's foolproof

contents

thanks

I love writing cookbooks and I'm so grateful to the wonderful people who work with me. First and foremost, I couldn't get through the day without my amazing "home team" of Barbara Libath, Suzanna Guiliano, and Erica Katz. They keep me sane and giggling all day long.

For the books, thank you to my publisher, Clarkson Potter, headed by my friend Pam Krauss, plus editor Rica Allannic, book designer Marysarah Quinn, and publicist Kate Tyler. I've been at Clarkson Potter since my first book and I love them all. I'm so proud of the quality of the books we produce together; they make me look so much better than I am.

My photographic team and I have been together for a long time—Quentin Bacon taking such beautiful photographs, Cyd McDowell artfully styling all the food, and now we have the happy addition of Barb Fritz, who brings us the most elegant props to play with. I love the weeks we spend together. Thank you also to my friend Sarah Chase, who inspires me with wonderful ideas, and to John Hall, for beautiful garden photographs.

There's also a team behind the scenes that is so important to me. Esther Newberg, my agent, brilliantly takes care of business, and Amelia Durand is extraordinary handling the demands of publicity. Thank you both so much.

But most of all, my sweet husband, Jeffrey, who is such a good sport on my TV show (yes, he's my real husband—not my TV husband). I could never have done a day of this without his loving encouragement and support.

introduction

I love when people stop me in the street or at a book signing and tell me they love my recipes because they're foolproof. I love to cook—I find it really satisfying—but between you and me, it's not always easy. Between the shopping, the cooking, and cleaning up it can be hard work to actually get dinner on the table. Why go to all that trouble only to find that the result is ho-hum or, worse, that the recipe doesn't work at all?

That's exactly why I wrote this book. Foolproof means so many things to me. Clearly, it means the recipe works—that goes without saying. But there's more to it than that. It's a dish that's deeply satisfying to eat; it's a company-friendly meal that can be made in advance to reduce your stress; and it's an outrageously delicious dessert that's so easy to make that it becomes part of your regular repertoire. I want these all to be the recipes that you love so much that you make them over and over again because *that's* when a recipe becomes truly foolproof: when you feel that you can almost make it with your eyes closed.

I think many people have the impression that a recipe is a simple engineering problem and that a dish should come out exactly the same way every time we make it. But as any cook will tell you, cooking is more like driving a car than constructing something: a thousand things can influence the outcome. Once you have some confidence and experience under your belt, you make all kinds of small adjustments along the way, and you do it without even thinking because you've done it so many times before. The potatoes are a little bigger than last time so you know they take a little longer to cook. The tomatoes aren't quite as ripe as you'd hoped so you choose to serve them roasted rather than sliced fresh. The oven isn't *really* a consistent 350 degrees but rather it fluctuates and you might need to turn it to 375 degrees to make sure the chicken browns the way you like. And then there's my particular annoyance: the steaks you asked the butcher to cut 1¼ inches thick are actually only ¾ inch thick—or even worse, some are 1 inch and some are 1½ inches. Aarrggh! But since I've had that problem before, I know that I'll want to put some of the steaks on the grill earlier than the others and to test them with an instant-read meat thermometer to be sure they're all done to exactly the right internal temperature.

But the best news is that I've made all of these recipes dozens of times before. I've highlighted all the speed bumps and the blind spots along the way so you can make the adjustments you need to make as you go along. That way, you can get the recipes right not just the first time but every time you make them.

foolproof recipes

Foremost, the value of a cookbook comes down to its recipes. Here's how I write a recipe to ensure that it will come out perfectly each time and that it's so delicious that your family says, "You made this *yourself*?" You'll never find an instruction in one of my recipes that says, "Getting the right consistency can be tricky" or "Stir every 5 minutes for 2 hours." I write recipes that have ingredients you can find at your local food store (with a few special exceptions

like truffle butter, which you can order online and keep in the freezer), that use the standard equipment you already have, over and over again, and that have cooking processes that are familiar. Hopefully, I've anticipated your questions and the answer is right there in the instructions. In fact, I've called out many of the tripping points to alert you. For example, for the Crispy English Potatoes (page 185), I noted "Roast . . . for 45 minutes, tossing occasionally, until they are very browned and crisp." Now you know about how long it should take *and* what to look for when it's done. Often, I'll tell you what to look for at a critical step. For the Sticky Toffee Date Cake (page 220) there's that moment when the mixture bubbles up violently, but you'll be prepared because I warned you in advance—so you'll know you're on the path to the perfect cake. (In fact, there are two scary parts to that recipe. The batter is also much thinner than any cake batter I've ever made, but because I tell you what to expect, you won't be worried that the consistency is off.) For each recipe in this book, I've tried to include markers along the way to let you know when you've nailed the process so you can proceed to the next step with total confidence.

foolproof shopping

It's easy to say "Have a well-stocked pantry," but who actually does? When I'm having a party, I plan the menu a week ahead of time so I can shop for the shelf goods and refrigerated ingredients like eggs and butter a few days before I get down to the cooking. Then, on the day before the party, when I already have too much to do, I have just a short list of things like fish and fresh herbs to pick up at the store.

It's really important to buy the right ingredients for a recipe. Once in a while, someone writes to me to say they made my chocolate cake and it didn't come out right—and what's wrong with my recipe? I'll quiz them and find out that oops! they didn't have any cocoa powder on hand so they used sardines instead. (That's probably not a good idea!) The first time you make a recipe, it's important to follow the instructions *exactly*. The next time you can make adjustments for your own taste. Of course, there are always small things you can change without a problem— like using semisweet chocolate instead of bittersweet, or a little less sugar than is called for—but you shouldn't expect to have the recipe come out right (or have it come out at all!) if you substitute something entirely different.

All through this book I've told you what my favorite ingredients are. It doesn't mean that I've tried every olive oil on the market, or that the recipe will only work with that brand; just that this is the one I use all the time and the recipe comes out with just the flavor I'm looking for. But only you know what you like best. Try it my way once and then if you'd like it spicier, sweeter, saltier—by all means, tweak the recipe the next time to make it yours.

foolproof entertaining

Most people can make one dish by itself, but for a party we often need to make several dishes. So that's why for me, a foolproof meal is about more than great recipes; it's also about planning a menu. Most of us find it daunting to get everything to the table—hot!—all at the same time. Each time I do a party, I write myself a "game plan" for how to organize the cooking so everything is ready at the moment I want to serve dinner. I've included my system in this book so you can make your own game plan each time you entertain. Once you know the system, it's actually not complicated; and I promise you'll never attack a party menu again without one. Instead of worrying about how it's all going to get done in time, all I do is glance at my game plan and realize I have nothing to do until, say, five P.M., and dinner will be ready promptly at eight o'clock. Nothing reduces stress for me more than a good game plan!

My wonderful assistant Barbara's son Jason got married this year and Barbara offered to host the rehearsal dinner. As the date got closer, she admitted to me that she was in a full-blown panic. We all know *that* feeling! I said, let's sit down and figure out how to do this in a way that won't either break the bank or send you into a tailspin.

First, we talked about the menu. Instead of having the party catered, which would have been expensive, Barbara and I made a list of all the delicious prepared foods she could buy locally that she could serve buffet-style. She ordered spicy brisket sandwiches and smoky baked beans from Townline BBQ in Sagaponack, New York, plus huge pots of New England clam chowder and lobster rolls from the Seafood Shop in Wainscott. Barbara and I then supplemented the list with easy things we could make like guacamole, vegetable coleslaw, and tarragon potato salad. Finally, Barbara's daughter Rebecca offered to make a huge sheet cake for the prewedding dinner. Barbara admitted that once we broke the menu into small bites, the party didn't seem nearly so overwhelming.

At the end of the day, foolproof is really about cooking with confidence. I hope that as you cook your way through this book you'll feel as though we're taking a little journey together. You're cooking and I'm standing quietly next to you ready to answer any question that you might have along the way. As I said, it's a little like driving a car. Everyone can do it, and as with driving, the more experience you have, the more easily you'll make the small adjustments along the way that ensure success. I hope in this book you'll find lots of foolproof recipes and easy ideas that help you cook with more confidence than you've ever felt in the kitchen.

xxx's Ina

10 foolproof tips for cooking

1. Read the entire recipe before you start cooking. You don't want to discover the beans need to soak overnight when guests are due to arrive in an hour.

2. Follow the recipe precisely when you make it the first time. After that, you can always modify it to your personal taste.

3. Buy the right ingredients. Using table salt instead of kosher salt or crushed tomatoes instead of whole tomatoes can really change a recipe.

4. Set most of the ingredients out on the counter before you start cooking so you don't run around like a crazy person or forget to add something to the recipe.

5. Unless you're Julia Child or an Iron Chef, measure *all* your ingredients. Use wet measures (glass measuring cups) for wet ingredients and dry measures (cups and teaspoons) for dry ingredients. I also use a small kitchen scale, which is a great tool for measuring.

6. Smell or taste ingredients for freshness before adding them to a recipe. Using fish, eggs, milk, or olive oil that are even slightly off can wreck even the most carefully made dish.

7. Taste for seasonings while you're cooking to see how the dish is progressing—except, obviously, things like raw chicken and hot caramel!

8. Grind your own black peppercorns and Parmesan cheese. It's amazing what a difference it makes.

9. Don't walk away from something simmering on the stove. While you're not looking, liquids can boil over or evaporate and ruin a perfectly good dish. Check them every 5 minutes or so to be sure the heat's right.

10. Store all food well, both raw ingredients and cooked dishes. Keep fresh meats and fish very cold and keep vegetables wrapped or in the crisper in your fridge. Allow cooked dishes to cool to room temperature and then wrap them tightly—and label them!—before storing in the refrigerator or freezer.

cocktails

dukes cosmopolitan

mustard & gruyère batons

caramelized bacon

sidecars with dried cherries

crab strudels

jalapeño cheddar crackers

rossinis

parmesan crisps

tuscan mashed chickpeas

chili tortilla chips

thyme-roasted marcona almonds

foolproof game plans

When friends come to my house for dinner, they're always surprised to find that I've written out a very specific game plan for preparing the meal. Someone recently said, "I always keep that in my head and it's so hard to remember. It never occurred to me to write it down!" My game plan is excruciatingly detailed; it literally starts with "5:30 P.M.—turn the oven to 350 degrees" and goes through all the steps, including "7:30 P.M. serve cocktails," and "8:15 P.M. serve dinner." A game plan is the answer for anyone like me who can't figure out how to get three hot things to the table all at the same time.

This is what I do: I study each recipe carefully and break it into small steps: prep time, cook time, and resting time. Say I'm serving Mustard-Marinated Flank Steak, Couscous with Peas & Mint, and Orange-Braised Carrots & Parsnips. The steak needs to marinate in the fridge for at least 2 hours, then it comes to room temperature for 30 minutes, goes onto the grill for 10 minutes, it rests under foil for 10 minutes. If I'm serving dinner at 8:15 P.M., that means I'll need to start the steak about 3 hours earlier, so I'll write, "5:00 P.M. prep flank steak" and "5:15 P.M. steak into fridge to marinate, 7:15 P.M. steak out of fridge and light grill, 7:45 P.M. grill steak, and 7:55 P.M. rest steak under foil." This chart actually does two things for me: first, I'm confident that I'll get the steak done at the right time for us to sit down for dinner at 8:15 P.M., but even more importantly, at 1 P.M., when I'm panicked that I should start cooking, I look at my game plan and realize there's nothing to do until 5:00 P.M.

Next, I'll put the vegetables into the game plan. Orange-Braised Carrots & Parsnips cook for an hour and a half, so I'll add those details to the schedule: "turn oven to 275 degrees," "prep carrots and parsnips," "put vegetables in oven," and "take vegetables out of oven." Couscous with Peas & Mint is prepped in advance and then needs to steam for 10 minutes before dinner, so that goes into the plan, too.

This is what this game plan looks like on paper:

5:00	**Prep steak marinade**
5:15	**Marinate steak and refrigerate**
6:30	**Prep carrots and parsnips**
	Prep couscous ingredients
	Turn oven to 275 degrees
6:45	**Put carrots and parsnips in oven**
7:15	**Take steak out of fridge**
	Light charcoal grill
7:30	**Guests arrive; serve wine and**
	Marcona almonds
7:45	**Grill steak**
	Heat couscous stock
7:55	**Rest steak under foil**
	Steam couscous
8:15	**Take vegetables out of oven**
	Serve dinner

There's another really important detail to this game plan. If I want to be sure I can actually execute a menu, not only will I choose dishes that can be prepared almost entirely before guests arrive, but I'll also be sure I haven't chosen three dishes that all go into the oven at the same time—and at three different temperatures! This menu has one thing prepared in the oven, one thing on top of the stove, and one on the grill. No problem! There's nothing on this chart that I don't feel totally comfortable doing in the time allotted. They're recipes I feel confident cooking because I've done them before, and with this game plan I know that dinner will be served—with everything hot—at 8:15 P.M., exactly as planned. How great is that?

dukes cosmopolitan

MAKES 4 DRINKS

Friends of mine introduced me to this delicious variation of the classic Cosmopolitan, which is from Dukes, the elegant London hotel and bar. The two things that make it special are freshly squeezed lemon juice, and a dash of egg white to make the drink frothy when you shake it.

- 4 ounces freshly squeezed lemon juice (2 lemons)
- 4 ounces Cointreau liqueur
- 7 ounces cranberry juice cocktail, such as Ocean Spray
- 7 ounces good vodka, such as Grey Goose
- Dash of raw egg white (optional)
- Ice

In a pitcher, stir together the lemon juice, Cointreau, cranberry juice cocktail, vodka, and egg white (if using). Fill a cocktail shaker half full with ice and pour enough of the drink mixture into the shaker to almost fill it. Shake the cocktail for a full 30 seconds (it's longer than you think!) and strain into martini glasses. Serve ice cold.

If you want frosty glasses, put the glasses in the freezer 30 minutes before serving.

You can prepare the mixture early in the day and refrigerate. Shake with ice and serve.

mustard & gruyère batons

MAKES 10 TO 12 BATONS

This was inspired by a recipe in my friend Dorie Greenspan's wonderful cookbook Around My French Table. *Frozen puff pastry is what makes these so easy—you can prepare the batons a day ahead, keep them in the fridge, and bake them before serving. The batons are flavored with spicy mustard and sharp Gruyère.*

Flour for dusting the board
1 **sheet of frozen puff pastry, thawed and very cold (see note)**
3 **tablespoons Dijon mustard**
1 **egg beaten with 1 teaspoon water, for egg wash**
3 **ounces Gruyère cheese, grated**
2 **tablespoons freshly grated Parmesan cheese**
Flaked sea salt, such as Maldon, for sprinkling

I use Pepperidge Farm frozen puff pastry. Defrost it overnight in the refrigerator.

To make ahead, refrigerate unbaked batons for up to 24 hours, and bake before serving.

Unfold the sheet of puff pastry on a well-floured board, and roll it to an 11 × 13-inch rectangle with a floured rolling pin. (Diagonal strokes keep the pastry rectangular.) With a shorter end closest to you, brush the lower half of the pastry evenly with the mustard, leaving a ½-inch border around the edges. Brush the border of the pastry with the egg wash and fold the top half over the bottom half, lining up the edges. Place the pastry on a sheet pan lined with parchment paper and chill for 15 minutes.

Place the pastry on a board and trim the three irregular edges with a sharp knife. With the folded edge away from you, cut the pastry in 1 × 6-inch strips. You will have 10 to 12 batons. Spread the batons out on the sheet pan so they're not touching. Brush the tops lightly with the egg wash (don't allow the egg wash to drip down the sides) and sprinkle evenly with the Gruyère, Parmesan, and 1½ teaspoons sea salt. Chill for at least 15 minutes.

When ready to bake, preheat the oven to 400 degrees.

Bake the batons for 15 to 18 minutes, until golden brown and puffed. Allow to cool on the pan for 3 minutes and serve warm.

caramelized bacon

MAKES 15 TO 20 HORS D'OEUVRES

This is the most outrageous hors d'oeuvre I've ever made and maybe the most addictive. The pieces of bacon are sweet and spicy and, believe it or not, they're delicious with a cocktail.

½ cup light brown sugar, lightly packed

½ cup chopped or whole pecans

2 teaspoons kosher salt

1 teaspoon freshly ground black pepper

¹⁄₈ teaspoon ground cayenne pepper

2 tablespoons pure maple syrup

½ pound thick-sliced applewood-smoked bacon, such as Nodine's

Preheat the oven to 375 degrees. Line a sheet pan with aluminum foil (for easy cleaning) and place a wire baking rack on top.

Combine the brown sugar and pecans in a food processor and process until the pecans are finely ground. Add the salt, black pepper, and cayenne pepper and pulse to combine. Add the maple syrup and pulse again to moisten the crumbs.

Cut each bacon slice in half crosswise and line up the pieces on the baking rack without touching. With a small spoon, evenly spread the pecan mixture on top of each piece of bacon, using all of the mixture. Bake for 25 to 30 minutes, until the topping is very browned but not burnt. If it's underbaked, the bacon won't crisp as it cools.

While it's hot, transfer the bacon to a plate lined with paper towels and set aside to cool. Serve at room temperature.

These can be made early in the day and stored at room temperature.

sidecars with dried cherries

MAKES 2 DRINKS

I've tried all kinds of sidecars but none of them really hit the spot. They're either too sour from the lemon, too sweet from the orange liqueur, or too harsh from inexpensive brandy. But I've always been intrigued because they seem to be a second cousin to my favorite drink—the whiskey sour. I decided to tackle the recipe (I know, my job is grueling) and came up with my version, which I think hits all the right notes. I use good but obviously not the best Cognac.

Juice of 1 lemon for sugaring the glasses
¼ cup sugar
¼ cup dried cherries
6 ounces good Cognac (VS not VSOP), divided
3 ounces freshly squeezed lemon juice (2 lemons)
3 ounces Grand Marnier liqueur
Ice

To sugar the glass rims, pour the juice of 1 lemon into a shallow bowl and put the sugar on a small plate. Dip the rim of 2 highball or martini glasses first in the lemon juice and then in the sugar. Set them aside to dry.

In a small bowl, combine the dried cherries with 2 ounces of the Cognac and microwave on high for 60 seconds. Set aside.

Combine the 3 ounces of lemon juice with the remaining 4 ounces of Cognac, the Grand Marnier, and 1 teaspoon of the marinated cherry liquid. Fill a cocktail shaker three-quarters full with ice and pour in the cocktail mixture. Shake the mixer for a full 30 seconds (it's longer than you think!) and strain into the prepared glasses either straight up or over ice. Thread 3 or 4 marinated cherries on small skewers and serve each drink ice cold with a skewer of cherries.

crab strudels

SERVES 8

For entertaining, savory strudels are terrific because they can be made in advance and frozen unbaked. This recipe was inspired by an hors d'oeuvre my friend Devon Fredericks used to make when she owned the wonderful specialty food store Loaves & Fishes in Sagaponack, New York. These strudels are filled with lots of succulent crabmeat and lightly seasoned with garlic, curry, and lime.

12 tablespoons (1½ sticks) unsalted butter, divided

3 scallions, white and green parts, chopped

2 teaspoons minced garlic (2 cloves)

1 teaspoon good curry powder

1 pound fresh lump crabmeat, drained and picked over to remove shells

1 tablespoon chopped fresh flat-leaf parsley

⅓ cup freshly squeezed lime juice (2 limes)

Kosher salt and freshly ground black pepper

15 sheets of phyllo dough, defrosted (see note)

Plain dry bread crumbs

Flaked sea salt, such as Maldon, for sprinkling

Defrost the phyllo dough overnight in the refrigerator.

Preheat the oven to 400 degrees. Line a sheet pan with parchment paper.

Heat 2 tablespoons of the butter in a medium (10-inch) sauté pan, add the scallions, and cook over medium-low heat for 5 minutes, until the scallions are tender. Add the garlic and curry powder and cook for 1 more minute.

Meanwhile, shred the crabmeat into a bowl and mix in the parsley, lime juice, 1½ teaspoons salt, and ½ teaspoon pepper. Stir in the scallion mixture.

Melt the remaining 10 tablespoons of butter in the same sauté pan. Unfold 1 sheet of the phyllo dough on a board with a long edge facing you. Brush the sheet generously with melted butter and sprinkle with ½ tablespoon bread crumbs. Repeat the process, layering phyllo, butter, and bread crumbs until you have 5 sheets piled up. (Place a lightly damp towel on the remaining phyllo to keep it pliable.) Spoon a third of the crab mixture on the edge of the long side of the phyllo and roll the dough tightly around the crabmeat, making sure the roll is even and round. Place on the sheet pan with the seamside down. Repeat the entire process until all the crabmeat is used. Brush the tops and sides of the strudels with melted butter and sprinkle with sea salt. With a small sharp knife, score the strudels diagonally at 1½-inch intervals and bake for 12 to 15 minutes, until the strudels are nicely browned. Slice along the scored lines and serve warm.

jalapeño cheddar crackers

MAKES 32 TO 34 CRACKERS

I make several rolls of this savory shortbread dough in advance, freeze them, and defrost them overnight in the refrigerator. All I have to do before the party is slice and bake. Sharp cheddar, jalapeño pepper, and chipotle chili powder make these spicy and delicious!

- 2 cups all-purpose flour
- 1 teaspoon kosher salt
- 1/8 teaspoon baking powder
- 14 tablespoons (1¾ sticks) cold unsalted butter, ½-inch-diced
- 5 ounces extra-sharp white Cheddar, grated
- 1 tablespoon minced seeded jalapeño pepper
- ¼ teaspoon chipotle chili powder
- 3 tablespoons ice water
- 1 egg beaten with 1 tablespoon milk, for egg wash
  Fleur de sel or sea salt

Place the flour, kosher salt, and baking powder in a food processor fitted with the steel blade and pulse to mix. Add the butter and pulse until the mixture resembles coarse meal. Add the Cheddar, jalapeño, and chipotle chili powder and pulse again. With the food processor running, add the ice water all at once. Continue pulsing until the mixture begins to form a ball. Dump the dough onto a floured board and roll it into a 14-inch log. Wrap in plastic, and refrigerate for at least 1 hour.

The unbaked rolls keep for 2 weeks in the refrigerator and for up to 6 months in the freezer. Defrost before baking.

When ready to bake, preheat the oven to 400 degrees. Line a sheet pan with parchment paper.

Cut the dough in 3/8-inch-thick slices. Place the crackers on the prepared sheet pan, brush with the egg wash, and sprinkle with the fleur de sel. Bake for 12 to 15 minutes, until golden brown. Serve slightly warm or at room temperature.

rossinis

MAKES 6 TO 7 DRINKS

I love Bellinis, which are made with Prosecco and fresh peach purée, so I thought it would be fun to find a new Prosecco cocktail. When the strawberries are ripe, these are divine. A dash of Grand Marnier makes the strawberries even sweeter.

 1 **pint (2 cups) ripe strawberries, hulled**
2½ **tablespoons sugar syrup (see note)**
 1 **teaspoon Grand Marnier liqueur**
 6 **orange zest strips, for garnish**
 1 **(750-ml) bottle Prosecco, chilled**

Place the strawberries in the bowl of a food processor fitted with the steel blade and purée until completely smooth. Pour the liquid through a fine-mesh sieve and press to make a seedless purée. Discard the seeds. Add the sugar syrup and Grand Marnier to the purée and refrigerate until very cold.

When ready to serve, rub the rim of each glass with the orange zest. Pour the cold Prosecco into Champagne glasses until they're each three-quarters full. Carefully stir 2 tablespoons of the purée into each glass and serve very cold.

To make sugar syrup, boil 1 cup sugar with 1 cup water until the sugar dissolves completely and chill. The syrup will last for a few weeks in the refrigerator.

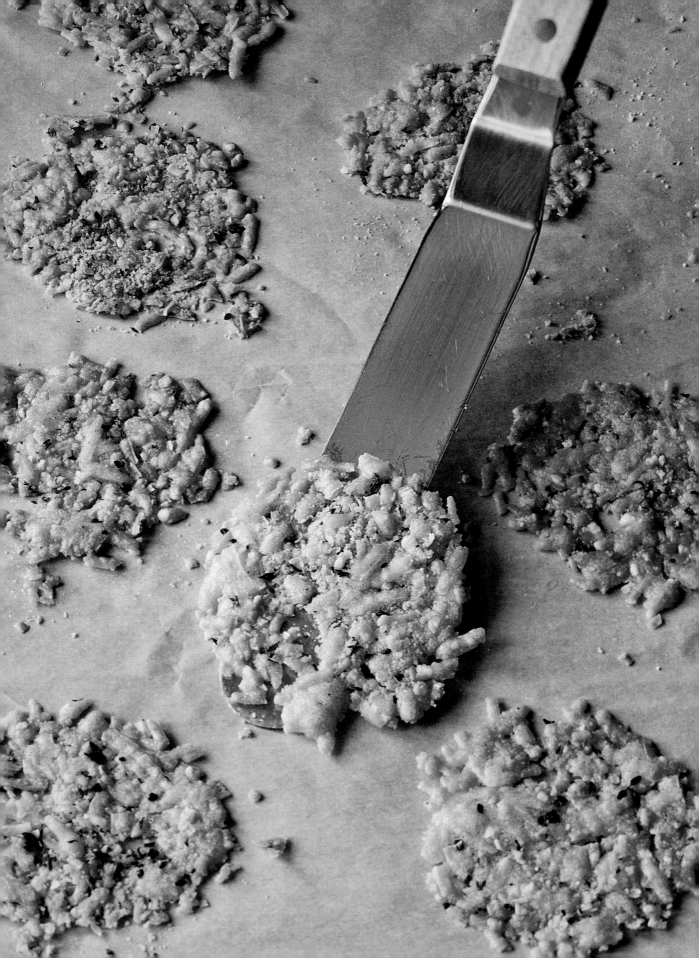

parmesan crisps

MAKES 15 CRISPS

This simplest of recipes—called frico—is one of the most elegant Italian delicacies you can serve with cocktails. It's nothing more than grated Parmesan cheese mixed with a little flour and fresh thyme and baked into crisps. Make a lot, because everyone will love them.

- 1 (4-ounce) piece of Parmesan Reggiano cheese (without the rind)
- 1 tablespoon all-purpose flour
- 1 teaspoon minced fresh thyme leaves
- ½ teaspoon kosher salt
- ½ teaspoon freshly ground black pepper

Preheat the oven to 350 degrees. Line 2 sheet pans with parchment paper.

Grate the Parmesan, using the large grating side of a box grater, as you might use to grate carrots. Combine the Parmesan, flour, thyme, salt, and pepper in a bowl and mix well. With a measuring spoon, spoon level tablespoons of the mixture onto the prepared sheet pans, spreading each round into a 3-inch disk. Toss the mixture each time and scoop from the bottom of the bowl to be sure you get some flour in each spoonful. Bake in the middle of the oven for 8 to 10 minutes, until golden brown.

Cool on the pans for 5 minutes, loosen with a metal spatula, then cool completely on a baking rack. Serve at room temperature.

These can be made a few days in advance, cooled completely, and stored between layers of parchment paper at room temperature in a sealed container.

tuscan mashed chickpeas

SERVES 6 TO 8

Canned chickpeas are a real time-saver. Purée them in a food processor with lots of seasonings like garlic, lemon juice, and Parmesan, and you have a hearty spread to serve with grilled bread. This is even better made in advance; the bread can be grilled just before serving.

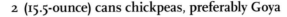

2 (15.5-ounce) cans chickpeas, preferably Goya
½ cup chicken stock, preferably homemade (page 62)
3 tablespoons good olive oil, plus extra for serving
2 ripe medium-size tomatoes, seeded and small-diced
2 garlic cloves, minced (see note)
¼ cup freshly grated Parmesan cheese (see note)
3 tablespoons minced fresh flat-leaf parsley
2 tablespoons freshly squeezed lemon juice
Kosher salt and freshly ground black pepper
Grilled country bread, for serving (see note)

Grating garlic on a Microplane is a fast alternative to mincing.

When a recipe calls for "grated" Parmesan, I grind it in a food processor fitted with the steel blade.

To grill bread, heat a gas or charcoal grill and toast the bread for 2 minutes on each side, until it's lightly browned.

Pour the chickpeas into a colander and rinse them under cold running water. Drain well. Place the chickpeas in the bowl of a food processor fitted with the steel blade. Add the chicken stock and pulse until the chickpeas are coarsely chopped but not puréed.

In a medium (10-inch) sauté pan, heat the 3 tablespoons of olive oil over medium heat. Add the tomatoes and sauté for 3 to 4 minutes, until the tomatoes are softened. Add the garlic and cook for 1 minute more. Add the chickpeas, stirring to combine with the tomatoes and garlic. Cook for about 5 minutes, stirring occasionally, until heated through. Off the heat, stir in the Parmesan, parsley, lemon juice, 2 teaspoons salt, and 1 teaspoon pepper and taste for seasonings. Pile in a serving bowl, drizzle with olive oil, and serve warm or at room temperature with shards of grilled country bread.

chili tortilla chips

SERVES 4

At Barefoot Contessa, Parker Hodges made homemade corn chips for parties and people went crazy. Nothing that comes in a bag and is made with artificial flavors can hold a candle to the real thing. When I have friends over, I like to set everything up at the stove and fry these while we enjoy our cocktails. Chipotle chili powder, chili powder, and cumin hit all the right notes.

    48 ounces (6 cups) peanut oil
    10 (6-inch) corn tortillas
     1 tablespoon kosher salt
    ¼ teaspoon chipotle chili powder
    ¼ teaspoon chili powder
    ¼ teaspoon ground cumin

It's important that the spices be sprinkled on while the chips are hot.

Pour the peanut oil into a large (11-inch-round × 4-inch-deep) stainless-steel pot fitted with a candy thermometer; you want the oil to be at least 1 inch deep. Heat the oil to about 380 degrees, or almost smoking. Cut the tortillas in quarters (they will seem large) and add them in batches to the hot oil without crowding them. Cook for 2 to 3 minutes, turning once to brown evenly. Remove the tortillas with a flat wire strainer or tongs and place them on a sheet pan lined with paper towels. Continue cooking the chips until they're all fried.

Meanwhile, combine the salt, chipotle chili powder, chili powder, and cumin in a small bowl. While the chips are still hot, sprinkle them evenly with the spice mixture. Serve warm or at room temperature.

thyme-roasted marcona almonds

SERVES 6 TO 8

My friend Eli Zabar always inspires me. He makes these almonds at his wonderful store Eli's Manhattan and they're so delicious that I tried them myself. Marcona almonds from Spain are expensive, but they're really worth it. Don't scrimp on the thyme or salt in this recipe—the almonds need both of them to have lots of flavor.

1 pound roasted, salted Marcona almonds
2 teaspoons good olive oil
2 tablespoons minced fresh thyme leaves
1 teaspoon kosher salt
1 teaspoon fleur de sel

Store the cooled nuts in a sealed container at room temperature for a week or two.

Preheat the oven to 350 degrees.

Place the almonds, olive oil, thyme, and kosher salt on a sheet pan and toss them together. Roast the almonds for 10 to 15 minutes, turning them every 5 minutes with a metal spatula, until they're lightly browned. Watch them carefully; they go from underbaked to burnt very quickly.

Sprinkle with the fleur de sel, toss, and set aside to cool. Serve warm or at room temperature.

starters

winter minestrone
& garlic bruschetta

easy tomato soup
& grilled cheese croutons

spanish pea soup with crispy ham

homemade chicken stock

easy gazpacho
& goat cheese croutons

tomato crostini with whipped feta

endive, orange &
roquefort salad

mussels with saffron mayonnaise

marinated artichoke hearts

fig & fennel caponata

easy tzatziki with feta

foolproof starters

One of the hardest things I find when making a dinner party is serving a first course. The nice thing about a starter is that it makes the meal more relaxed; it stretches dinner out over a longer time. Without it, you serve dinner and dessert and bam!—the evening's over and it's only 9:30 P.M. As the hostess, it's my job to orchestrate the flow of the party and when I serve a first course, the evening feels a little more luxurious and leisurely. Plus, there are so many starters that I really love.

A first course can be something simple like a cold salad that's already done or a soup that's simmering away on top of the stove. That's not the problem. The problem is the main course—how do I get it ready while I'm casually enjoying my soup and entertaining my friends? The main course often has to be carved, finished, and plated, which takes time and finesse while everyone's sitting at the kitchen table watching me.

The key to serving a first course without totally stressing yourself out is to choose a main course that can be either completely done or close to done before you sit down to dinner. For example, the Four-Hour Lamb can be sitting in the oven staying warm at a low temperature, the Filet of Beef with Basil Parmesan Mayonnaise can be resting under a tent of aluminum foil, or the sauce for the Penne alla Vecchia Bettola can be ready and waiting to be poured onto the pasta. Once the first-course plates are cleared, all I'll have to do is put the main course out—slice the meat, toss the pasta, or just put a big ovenproof pot out on the buffet and dinner's served. Here's a tip: Ask one of your guests to help. They feel like they're on the A-team; they can open the wine, pick up salad plates, and help get dinner on the table.

winter minestrone & garlic bruschetta

SERVES 6 TO 8

This incredibly hearty winter soup falls somewhere between a soup and a stew. The texture and flavor are amazing—it's filled with chunky vegetables, pasta, beans, and spinach. Pesto and Parmesan swirled in at the end make it even better. I serve it in big shallow bowls with garlic bruschetta on top.

Good olive oil

4 ounces pancetta, ½-inch-diced

1½ cups chopped yellow onions

2 cups (½-inch) diced carrots (3 carrots)

2 cups (½-inch) diced celery (3 stalks)

2½ cups (½-inch) diced peeled butternut squash

1½ tablespoons minced garlic (4 cloves)

2 teaspoons chopped fresh thyme leaves

26 ounces canned or boxed chopped tomatoes, such as Pomi

6 to 8 cups chicken stock, preferably homemade (page 62)

1 bay leaf

Kosher salt and freshly ground black pepper

1 (15-ounce) can cannellini beans, drained and rinsed

2 cups cooked small pasta, such as tubetti (see note)

8 to 10 ounces fresh baby spinach leaves

½ cup good dry white wine

2 tablespoons store-bought pesto

Garlic Bruschetta (recipe follows)

Freshly grated Parmesan cheese, for serving

To cook the pasta, put 1 cup of pasta into a large pot of boiling salted water. Cook according to the directions on the package, drain, and set aside.

You can make this soup ahead and reheat it before serving. It will need to be reseasoned.

Heat 2 tablespoons of olive oil over medium heat in a large, heavy pot or Dutch oven. Add the pancetta and cook over medium-low heat for 6 to 8 minutes, stirring occasionally, until lightly browned. Add the onions, carrots, celery, squash, garlic, and thyme and cook over medium heat, stirring occasionally, for 8 to 10 minutes, until the vegetables begin to soften.

Add the tomatoes, 6 cups of the chicken stock, the bay leaf, 1 tablespoon salt, and 1½ teaspoons pepper to the pot. Bring to a boil, then lower the heat and simmer uncovered for 30 minutes, until the vegetables are tender.

Discard the bay leaf. Add the beans and cooked pasta and heat through. The soup should be quite thick but if it's *too* thick, add more chicken stock. Just before serving, reheat the soup, add the spinach, and toss with 2 big spoons (like tossing a salad). Cook just until the leaves are wilted. Stir in the white wine and pesto. Depending on the saltiness of the chicken stock, add another teaspoon or two of salt to taste. Serve large shallow bowls of soup with a bruschetta on top. Sprinkle with Parmesan cheese, drizzle with olive oil, and serve hot.

garlic bruschetta

1 baguette
Good olive oil
1 garlic clove, cut in half lengthwise

Preheat the oven to 425 degrees.

Slice the baguette at a 45-degree angle in ½-inch-thick slices. Brush both sides of the bread with olive oil and bake for 6 minutes, until lightly toasted. Take the slices out of the oven and rub the surface of each one with the cut clove of garlic.

easy tomato soup
& grilled cheese croutons

SERVES 4 TO 6

My friend Frank Newbold told me he'd been served tomato soup with grilled cheese croutons on top and I thought, OMG what a great idea! This tomato soup is spiced with saffron, which has enough flavor to stand up to the Gruyère in the croutons. Nursery food updated—how bad could that be?

3 tablespoons good olive oil

3 cups yellow onions, chopped (2 onions)

1 tablespoon minced garlic (3 cloves)

4 cups chicken stock, preferably homemade (page 62)

1 (28-ounce) can crushed tomatoes, preferably San Marzano

Large pinch of saffron threads

Kosher salt and freshly ground black pepper

½ cup orzo

½ cup heavy cream

Grilled Cheese Croutons (recipe follows)

You can make the soup ahead and reheat it before serving.

In a large pot or Dutch oven such as Le Creuset, heat the olive oil over medium heat. Add the onions and cook over medium-low heat for 15 minutes, stirring occasionally, until golden brown. Add the garlic and cook for 1 more minute. Stir in the chicken stock, tomatoes, saffron, 1 tablespoon salt, and 1 teaspoon pepper. Bring the soup to a boil, then lower the heat and simmer for 15 minutes.

Meanwhile, fill a medium pot with water, add 2 teaspoons salt, and bring to a boil. Add the orzo and cook for 7 minutes. (It will finish cooking in the soup.) Drain the orzo and add it to the soup. Stir in the cream, return the soup to a simmer, and cook for 10 more minutes, stirring frequently.

Serve hot with Grilled Cheese Croutons scattered on top.

grilled cheese croutons

SERVES 4 TO 6

These are very easy to make if you have an electric panini grill but, of course, you can always make them the traditional way in a frying pan.

> 4 (½-inch-thick) slices country white bread
> 2 tablespoons unsalted butter, melted
> 4 ounces Gruyère cheese, grated

Heat a panini grill. Place the four slices of bread on a cutting board and brush lightly with the melted butter, being sure to butter the corners. Turn the slices over and pile Gruyère on two of the slices. Place the remaining two slices of bread on top of the Gruyère, buttered sides up.

Grill the sandwiches on the panini grill for about 5 minutes, until nicely browned. Place on a cutting board, allow to rest for 1 minute, and cut into 1-inch cubes.

You can assemble the cheese sandwiches ahead but grill them just before serving.

spanish pea soup
with crispy ham

SERVES 6

This may be the fastest hot soup I've ever made—and one of the most delicious. Using peas directly from the freezer makes this soup foolproof; the shallots and ham give it lots of flavor.

Good olive oil
½ **cup chopped shallots (2 large shallots)**
1 **tablespoon minced garlic (3 cloves)**
4 **cups chicken stock, preferably homemade (page 62)**
2 **pounds frozen peas, such as Bird's Eye Sweet Garden**
  Kosher salt and freshly ground black pepper
6 **thin slices Spanish Serrano ham or Italian prosciutto**

In a deep (8 × 5-inch) heavy-bottomed saucepan, heat 2 tablespoons of olive oil over medium heat. Add the shallots and sauté for 3 to 5 minutes, stirring occasionally, until tender and lightly browned. Add the garlic and cook for 1 more minute. Add the chicken stock, frozen peas, 2 teaspoons salt, and 1 teaspoon pepper and bring to a boil. Lower the heat and simmer for 5 minutes. Purée with an immersion blender until coarsely puréed. (I like it to have some texture.) Alternatively, use a blender to purée the soup 1 cup at a time. Pour the soup back into the pot and season to taste. Depending on the saltiness of the stock, I may add up to another teaspoon of salt and ½ teaspoon pepper to give the soup a very bright flavor.

Refrigerate this soup for a few days or freeze it for a few months.

Meanwhile, preheat the oven to 425 degrees. Place the ham in a single layer on a sheet pan and roast for 5 to 8 minutes, until crisp.

Reheat the soup and serve in shallow bowls with a slice of crispy ham on top. Drizzle with a little olive oil and serve hot.

homemade chicken stock

MAKES 6 QUARTS

I have to include this recipe in every book because it's the basis for so many of my dishes. Of course, you can use canned stock or broth; but this is easy to make and the difference in flavor is astonishing. When I'm at home, I throw everything into a big pot and let it simmer away for 4 hours. The house smells wonderful.

- 3 (5-pound) roasting chickens
- 3 large yellow onions, unpeeled and quartered
- 6 carrots, unpeeled and halved crosswise
- 4 celery stalks with leaves, cut into thirds crosswise
- 4 parsnips, unpeeled and halved crosswise (optional)
- 20 sprigs fresh flat-leaf parsley
- 15 sprigs fresh thyme
- 20 sprigs fresh dill
- 1 head garlic, unpeeled and cut in half crosswise
- 2 tablespoons kosher salt
- 2 teaspoons whole black peppercorns (not ground)

Place the chickens, onions, carrots, celery, parsnips, parsley, thyme, dill, garlic, salt, and peppercorns in a 16- to 20-quart stockpot. Add 7 quarts of water and bring it to a boil. Lower the heat and simmer uncovered for 4 hours, skimming off any foam that comes to the top. Set aside until cool enough to handle. Strain the entire contents of the pot through a colander and discard the solids. Pack the liquid in quart containers and refrigerate for a few days or freeze for up to 4 months.

easy gazpacho
& goat cheese croutons

SERVES 6

There's a small Spanish restaurant Jeffrey and I love near the Borough Market in London called Brindisa. We ordered a bowl of gazpacho and a platter of very thinly sliced Spanish ham for lunch. (There may have been a bottle of good Spanish wine in there, too.) When I made the soup at home, I added goat cheese croutons. Really good canned tomatoes not only make this dish easy to prepare, but it also means you can enjoy it even when tomatoes aren't in season.

Croutons look best when sliced on an angle.

I use San Marzano tomatoes.

2 (28-ounce) cans whole peeled tomatoes, drained (see note)

4 scallions

¼ seedless cucumber, unpeeled and seeds removed

1 large red onion

6 garlic cloves

½ cup red wine vinegar

½ cup good olive oil, plus extra for toasts and drizzling

½ teaspoon celery salt

¼ teaspoon crushed red pepper flakes

2 tablespoons tomato paste

1½ cups tomato juice, preferably Sacramento

Kosher salt and freshly ground black pepper

1 baguette

4 ounces garlic and herb goat cheese, such as Montrachet

Cut the tomatoes, scallions, cucumber, and onion in large pieces and place them in a food processor fitted with the steel blade. Add the garlic and pulse until the soup is coarsely puréed. Place it in a large bowl and whisk in the vinegar, olive oil, celery salt, red pepper flakes, tomato paste, tomato juice, 1 tablespoon salt, and 1½ teaspoons pepper. Cover with plastic wrap and chill for 4 hours or overnight.

When ready to serve, preheat the broiler and place the top rack 5 to 7 inches from the heat. Cut 6 (½-inch-thick) diagonal slices from the baguette. Place on a sheet pan, brush with olive oil, and broil for 1 to 2 minutes on one side. Turn the slices, spread with the goat cheese, and broil for another minute, until the cheese is warm and the bread is toasted. Serve big bowls of cold soup with a warm goat cheese crouton and a drizzle of olive oil.

tomato crostini
with whipped feta

SERVES 6 TO 8

I can't tell you how many times I've made this! The crisp toasts with lemony sharp feta and sweet ripe tomatoes are an unbeatable combination. I prep all the parts in advance and then just assemble them before dinner for a wonderful first course.

> 6 ounces good feta, crumbled
> 2 ounces cream cheese, at room temperature
> ⅔ cup good olive oil, divided
> 2 tablespoons freshly squeezed lemon juice
> Kosher salt and freshly ground black pepper
> 2 tablespoons minced shallots (2 shallots)
> 2 teaspoons minced garlic (2 cloves)
> 2 tablespoons good red wine vinegar
> 2 pounds ripe heirloom or cherry tomatoes, ½-inch-diced
> 3 tablespoons julienned fresh basil leaves, plus extra for serving
> 20 to 25 (½-inch-thick) diagonal baguette slices, toasted (see note)
> 2 tablespoons toasted pine nuts (page 169)

Place the bread slices on sheet pans, brush with olive oil, and bake at 425 degrees for 6 to 8 minutes, until lightly browned.

For the whipped feta, place the feta and cream cheese in the bowl of a food processor fitted with the steel blade. Pulse until the cheeses are mixed. Add ⅓ cup of the olive oil, the lemon juice, ½ teaspoon salt, and ¼ teaspoon pepper and process until smooth.

For the tomatoes, up to an hour before you're serving, combine the shallots, garlic, and vinegar in a medium bowl. Set aside for 5 minutes. Whisk in the remaining ⅓ cup olive oil, 1 teaspoon salt, and ½ teaspoon pepper. Add the tomatoes, stir gently, and set aside for 10 minutes. Stir in the basil and taste for seasonings.

To assemble the crostini, spread each slice of bread with a generous amount of whipped feta. With a slotted spoon, place the tomatoes on top. Put the crostini on plates and scatter with the pine nuts. Sprinkle with extra basil and serve.

endive, orange & roquefort salad

SERVES 6

In the winter, I look for salad ingredients that taste good all year long. This is the perfect layering of sweet orange and apple, spicy Roquefort cheese, and peppery arugula. It makes a great first course or a light lunch.

for the vinaigrette

½ teaspoon grated orange zest

¼ cup freshly squeezed orange juice

¼ cup good olive oil

1 teaspoon white wine vinegar

Kosher salt and freshly ground black pepper

for the salad

2 heads Belgian endive

½ cup walnut halves, toasted (see note)

¼ pound French Roquefort cheese, ½-inch-diced

1 sweet red apple, unpeeled, cored and medium-diced

4 ounces baby arugula

1 orange

Toast the walnuts in a dry sauté pan over low heat for 5 to 10 minutes, until lightly toasted.

You can make the vinaigrette ahead, refrigerate it, and assemble the salad just before serving.

In a small bowl, whisk together the orange zest, orange juice, olive oil, vinegar, 1 teaspoon salt, and $1/3$ teaspoon pepper. Set aside.

Cut the heads of endive in half lengthwise, remove the triangle of core at the base of each half so the leaves separate, and cut the leaves in half again lengthwise. Place in a large bowl. Drizzle the leaves with the vinaigrette and add the walnuts, Roquefort, and apple. Add the arugula and toss. Zest the orange into the salad with a strip zester. Peel the orange and remove the white pith around the orange with a small sharp knife. Cut the orange sections between the membranes and toss them on the salad. Discard the membranes. Sprinkle with salt and serve.

mussels
with saffron mayonnaise

SERVES 4 TO 5

I generally cook mussels in a garlicky broth and serve them as an entrée with big chunks of French bread to dip in the sauce. This is a totally different thing—these mussels are served as an appetizer family-style in a big cast-iron pot with a spicy saffron mayonnaise for dipping. Everyone pulls off the top shell, dips the mussel in the mayonnaise, and eats it "oyster style" from the bottom shell.

½ teaspoon saffron threads

⅔ cup good mayonnaise, such as Hellmann's

1 teaspoon grated lemon zest

1 tablespoon freshly squeezed lemon juice

1 teaspoon Dijon mustard

Kosher salt and freshly ground black pepper

¾ teaspoon fleur de sel or sea salt

1½ pounds mussels, cleaned (see note)

⅓ cup dry white wine

For the saffron mayonnaise, soak the saffron in 1 tablespoon hot water in a small bowl for 5 minutes. Whisk in the mayonnaise, lemon zest, lemon juice, mustard, ½ teaspoon kosher salt, and ¼ teaspoon pepper and refrigerate until ready to use.

For the mussels, combine the fleur de sel and ½ teaspoon pepper and set aside. Heat a large (12-inch), dry cast-iron skillet over high heat for 4 to 5 minutes, until very hot. Add the mussels in a single layer and cook them for 1 minute, until they start to open. Add the wine and continue cooking for 2 to 3 minutes, until the mussels are fully opened and just cooked. (Discard any that don't open.) Off the heat, sprinkle the mussels generously with the salt and pepper mixture. Serve hot from the skillet with individual bowls of saffron mayonnaise for dipping.

If you buy cultivated mussels, you'll just need to rinse them before cooking. Otherwise, pull off the "beards" with your fingers and soak them in water with a tablespoon of flour for about 20 minutes.

To serve more people, use two skillets; the mussels must cook in one layer.

marinated artichoke hearts

SERVES 6

This is a classic Provençal dish called artichokes barigoule. It's too time-consuming to trim fresh artichokes, and the frozen ones are actually delicious. Lemon, Pernod, garlic, olives, and basil make this dish really flavorful. I serve it as part of an antipasto platter or with a buffet of summer salads. Make it in advance to allow the flavors to develop.

I buy pancetta in a hunk and dice it myself.

Defrost frozen artichoke hearts overnight in the refrigerator.

¼ cup good olive oil

2 ounces pancetta, ¼-inch-diced

1 yellow onion, peeled and sliced into ¼-inch-thick rings

2 carrots, scrubbed and sliced into ¼-inch-thick rounds

3 (9-ounce) packages frozen artichoke hearts, defrosted (see note)

1 lemon, cut crosswise in ¼-inch-thick slices

2½ tablespoons Pernod liqueur

12 sun-dried tomatoes in oil, drained

3 garlic cloves, thinly sliced lengthwise

Kosher salt and freshly ground black pepper

½ cup green olives, such as picholine, for serving

3 tablespoons julienned fresh basil leaves

2 tablespoons freshly squeezed lemon juice

In a large (12- to 14-inch) pot, heat the olive oil over medium heat. Add the pancetta and cook for 2 to 3 minutes, until it renders some fat. Add the onions and carrots and cook for 5 to 7 minutes, stirring frequently, until tender but not browned. Arrange the artichokes on top of the vegetables. Add 2½ cups of water, the lemon slices, Pernod, sun-dried tomatoes, garlic, 1 tablespoon salt, and 1½ teaspoons pepper and bring to a boil. Lower the heat and simmer for 10 minutes, stirring occasionally. Turn off the heat and allow the artichokes to sit in the liquid until cooled.

When ready to serve, stir in the olives, basil, lemon juice, and 1 teaspoon salt. Serve the artichokes and other vegetables at room temperature or chilled, spooning some of the cooking liquid over each serving.

fig & fennel caponata

SERVES 6 TO 8

Caponata is a sweet and sour Sicilian condiment that's usually made with eggplant. I decided to do a twist on it with fennel, tomatoes, and figs. It's wonderful as a first course served on grilled shards of bread, but it's also good as a relish with grilled swordfish.

- 3 tablespoons good olive oil
- 1½ cups (½-inch) diced red onion
- 2 cups (½-inch) diced fennel (1 large)
- 3 garlic cloves, thinly sliced
- ⅓ cup good sherry vinegar
- 1 cup canned crushed tomatoes in pureé, such as Redpack
- 8 dried Calmyrna figs, stems removed and ¼-inch-diced
- 2½ tablespoons light brown sugar, lightly packed
- 2 tablespoons drained capers
- ½ cup green olives, pitted and coarsely chopped, such as Cerignola
- 1 teaspoon grated orange zest
- Kosher salt and freshly ground black pepper
- ⅓ cup freshly squeezed orange juice
- 3 tablespoons chopped fresh flat-leaf parsley
- Grilled bread for serving (page 42)

Heat the olive oil over medium heat in a medium (10-inch) sauté pan. Add the onions and fennel and sauté for 7 to 8 minutes, stirring occasionally, until softened. Add the garlic and cook for 1 more minute.

Stir in the vinegar, tomatoes, figs, and brown sugar, stirring to coat everything with the tomatoes. Stir in the capers, olives, orange zest, 1½ teaspoons salt, and ½ teaspoon pepper. Bring to a boil, then lower the heat, and simmer for 8 to 10 minutes, until thickened. Stir in the orange juice and parsley. Taste for seasonings; the caponata should be highly seasoned.

Serve the caponata warm or at room temperature with slices of the grilled bread.

Caponata can be made days in advance and stored in a sealed container in the refrigerator.

easy tzatziki with feta

SERVES 8

I love tzatziki, the garlicky Greek cucumber and yogurt dip. Traditionally, you drain the cucumbers and yogurt overnight in the refrigerator, but with thick Greek-style yogurt and hothouse cucumbers, you can skip that annoying step. I serve this as part of a first course, but it's also good with rack of lamb.

2 (7-ounce) containers Greek yogurt, such as Fage Total
1 hothouse cucumber, unpeeled
¼ cup sour cream
2 tablespoons freshly squeezed lemon juice
1 tablespoon white wine vinegar
1 tablespoon minced fresh dill
1½ teaspoons minced garlic (2 cloves)
Kosher salt and freshly ground black pepper

for serving

½ pound feta, sliced
Good olive oil
Fresh thyme leaves
½ pound large kalamata olives with pits
Toasted pita triangles (see note)

Tzatziki can be made a few days ahead and refrigerated.

Cut pita bread in triangles and toast in a 350-degree oven for 10 minutes.

Place the yogurt in a medium bowl. Grate the cucumber on a box grater on the largest grating side and squeeze it with your hands to remove most (but not all) of the liquid. Add the grated cucumber to the yogurt. Add the sour cream, lemon juice, vinegar, dill, garlic, 2 teaspoons salt, and ½ teaspoon pepper and combine. Taste for seasonings.

To serve, artfully arrange salad plates with slices of feta, drizzle them with olive oil, and sprinkle with thyme leaves. Add the olives, pita triangles, and the tzatziki and serve cold or at room temperature.

lunch

hot smoked salmon

italian seafood salad

lobster corn fritters

fennel & garlic shrimp

salmon & guacamole
sandwiches

lobster & potato salad

israeli couscous & tuna salad

balsamic roasted beet salad

roasted asparagus & prosciutto

white bean & arugula salad

foolproof menus

My friend Kristin Fisher is a very good cook but she confided to me one day that she has a hard time putting a menu together. It occurred to me that many people might have the same problem. I decided to give Kristin a birthday present: I went through all my cookbooks and put together my favorite foolproof menus for entertaining that I have relied on for years. They're the ones that I use over and over again because I know the dishes will come out perfectly every time.

Why do these menus work so well? First, the dishes are things that everyone loves to eat—not fancy, just simple, delicious food that you want to eat at home. Second, the recipes are easy enough to make that you can actually get three or four things to the table at the same time without driving yourself crazy. Many of the dishes—or at least a lot of the prep—can be done in advance. And finally, they're recipes that don't need six stockpots, two sauté pans, and four ovens at the same time. They're actually doable without a culinary education, which when I'm planning a meal for friends, is exactly what I'm looking for. I truly encourage you to assemble a portfolio of your own favorite recipes organized by meal. I put Kristin's recipes into a large artist's portfolio that allowed me to slide 8½ × 11-inch recipe pages into clear plastic sleeves. They were organized by menu but it was also very easy for her to add or change the recipes for her own dinner plans. For example, I included one of my all-time favorite menus—Chicken with Goat Cheese & Basil, Tagliarelle with Truffle Butter, and Roasted Carrots, plus French Apple Tart for dessert—because it's simple enough to serve as dinner for six but special enough to serve for New Year's Eve (which I've done!). I know that early in the day, I can stuff the chicken breasts and put them in the fridge, prep the carrots and leave them in water in the fridge, and bake the apple tart. When guests arrive, I can throw the chicken and carrots in the oven, make the pasta (it only takes ten minutes), and dinner's ready in no time. I'm totally relaxed, which is the best way to guarantee you'll have a fun party. There is a list of my favorite foolproof menus for entertaining on pages 264–265.

hot smoked salmon

SERVES 6

When I was a caterer, there was a man who made hot smoked salmon for me for parties and I've never forgotten it. The flavor was like smoked salmon, but it had the texture of poached salmon—it was so moist! I tried to re-create that dish for decades and I've finally done it. This can be served hot or cold.

- ¼ cup granulated sugar
- ¼ cup dark brown sugar, lightly packed
  Kosher salt
- 1 tablespoon coarsely ground black peppercorns
- 1 tablespoon grated lemon zest (2 lemons)
- 2 pounds King salmon fillets, skin on (whole or cut in serving pieces)
- 3 cups wood chips such as oak, hickory, or mesquite
  Charcoal
- 1 large, flat disposable foil pan
  Fresh Dill Sauce, for serving (recipe follows)

The night before serving, combine the granulated sugar, brown sugar, 2 tablespoons salt, the peppercorns, and lemon zest in a small bowl. Place the salmon fillets skin side down on a large flat ceramic or glass dish. Spread the mixture evenly on top of the salmon. Cover the dish with plastic wrap and refrigerate.

At least 1½ hours before you plan to cook the salmon, soak the wood chips in water.

Thirty minutes before you're ready to cook, heat the charcoal. Place a double layer of coals on one side of the grill, light them, and allow them to burn until the coals are gray on the outside. (I use a charcoal chimney to light the coals.) Sprinkle half the soaked wood chips on the hot coals (you will see lots of smoke). On the *other* side of the grill, place the foil pan and pour in 1 cup water. Place the cooking grate over the coals and the pan.

Scrape most of the sugar mixture off the salmon and sprinkle with 1 teaspoon of salt. Place the salmon skin side down on the side of the grill directly over the foil pan. Put the lid on the grill, making sure the top and bottom vents are open. Smoke the salmon for 10 minutes. Add the remaining wood chips directly on the coals and cook for 5 to 10 more minutes, depending on the thickness of the salmon, until it's firm to the touch and barely cooked. Don't overcook the salmon or it will be dry!

Transfer the salmon to a clean platter and immediately cover tightly with aluminum foil. Allow to rest for 10 minutes. Remove and discard the skin, if desired, and serve hot, at room temperature, or cold with the Fresh Dill Sauce.

fresh dill sauce

MAKES 2 CUPS

½ cup good mayonnaise, such as Hellmann's

½ cup sour cream

½ cup plain yogurt, such as Stonyfield

2 tablespoons cream cheese, at room temperature

½ cup chopped scallions, white and green parts (4 scallions)

½ cup minced fresh dill

¼ cup minced fresh flat-leaf parsley

1 teaspoon grated lemon zest

2 tablespoons freshly squeezed lemon juice

Kosher salt and freshly ground black pepper

1 cup seeded, grated hothouse cucumber

Place the mayonnaise, sour cream, yogurt, cream cheese, scallions, dill, parsley, lemon zest, lemon juice, 2 teaspoons salt, and 1 teaspoon pepper in the bowl of a food processor fitted with the steel blade. Purée for a few seconds, until well mixed. Add the cucumber and purée for another few seconds, until combined. Pour into a container and refrigerate for a few hours to allow the flavors to develop.

italian seafood salad

SERVES 6 TO 8

So many Italian restaurants have their own version of seafood salad and many of them are delicious. I decided to make one—with lots of fresh lemon juice and a splash of the Italian limoncello to really bring out the briny flavor of shellfish.

1 tablespoon Old Bay seasoning

Kosher salt

1½ pounds (16- to 20-count) peeled and deveined shrimp

1½ cups dry white wine

1 pound sea scallops, halved crosswise (see note)

1 pound cleaned fresh calamari, sliced crosswise in ½-inch-thick rings

2 pounds fresh mussels (see note)

½ cup good olive oil

4 teaspoons minced garlic (4 cloves)

2 teaspoons dried oregano

½ teaspoon crushed red pepper flakes

3 plum tomatoes, seeds and pulp removed and medium-diced

⅓ cup limoncello liqueur

Grated zest of 1 lemon

¼ cup freshly squeezed lemon juice (2 lemons)

Freshly ground black pepper

1 small fennel bulb, trimmed, cored, and thinly sliced crosswise

½ cup fresh flat-leaf parsley leaves, lightly packed

2 lemons

Scallops sometimes have a hard nub where they attached to the shell. Remove the nub with a small knife.

If you buy cultivated mussels, they'll already be clean. Otherwise, de-beard the mussels and soak in water with a tablespoon of flour for about 20 minutes.

Fill a large pot with 3 quarts of water and add the Old Bay seasoning and 1 tablespoon of salt. Bring to a boil, add the shrimp, lower the heat, and simmer for 3 minutes, until just firm. With a skimmer or slotted spoon, transfer the shrimp to a large bowl. Leave 2 cups of the poaching liquid in the pot and discard the rest.

Add the wine to the poaching liquid and bring to a boil. Add the scallops, lower the heat, and simmer for 2 minutes, until just cooked.

With the skimmer, transfer the scallops to the bowl with the shrimp. Bring the poaching liquid back to a boil, add the calamari, and simmer for 2 to 3 minutes, until just cooked. Be careful not to overcook any of the seafood or it will be tough! With the skimmer, transfer the calamari to the bowl.

Bring the poaching liquid to a boil again, add the mussels, cover, and simmer for 4 to 5 minutes, until all the shells have opened, discarding any that don't open. Turn off the heat and set aside until the mussels in the broth are cool enough to handle. Remove the mussels from the shells and add to the bowl. Add 12 of the shells to the seafood and discard the rest. Set aside ½ cup of the poaching liquid, discarding the rest. Drain the seafood in a colander and put it all back into the bowl.

Be sure there's no liquid in the bowl before pouring the dressing on the seafood or the liquid will dilute the flavor.

For the dressing, heat the olive oil in a medium (10-inch) sauté pan over medium heat. Add the garlic, oregano, and red pepper flakes and cook for 1 minute. (Be careful: Overcooked garlic will be bitter.) Add the tomatoes and cook over medium heat for 2 more minutes. Add the reserved poaching liquid, the limoncello, lemon zest, lemon juice, 1 tablespoon salt, and 1 teaspoon pepper and cook for 1 more minute. Pour the sauce over the seafood and toss gently. Add the fennel and parsley. Cut a lemon in half lengthwise, cut it thinly crosswise, and add it to the salad. Toss gently to combine and cover with plastic wrap. Chill for at least 3 hours or overnight.

To serve, sprinkle with 2 teaspoons salt, 1 teaspoon pepper, and the juice of the remaining lemon. Taste for seasonings and serve cold or at room temperature.

lobster corn fritters

MAKES 12 TO 14 FRITTERS; SERVES 4 TO 6

I love discovering new ingredients, as long as they're widely available. Unlike other red pepper sauces, sriracha is not so spicy that it overpowers the delicate lobster but it adds depth to the flavor of the corn. If you want to cook the lobsters yourself, 3 (1-pound) lobsters will yield 12 ounces of cooked meat.

Sriracha is a spicy Thai chili sauce that's made from sun-ripened chilies, which are ground together with garlic into a smooth paste and mixed with vinegar and seasonings.

6 to 8   tablespoons (¾ to 1 stick) unsalted butter
5   scallions, thinly sliced
1¼   cups fresh corn kernels (2 to 3 ears)
12   ounces freshly cooked lobster meat, ¼-inch-diced
1   cup all-purpose flour
1   teaspoon baking powder
1   teaspoon paprika
¾   teaspoon Old Bay seasoning
Kosher salt
2   extra-large eggs, lightly beaten
½   cup half-and-half

for the sauce

2   teaspoons minced garlic (2 cloves)
½   teaspoon saffron threads
2   teaspoons sriracha chili sauce
1   tablespoon freshly squeezed lemon juice
⅔   cup good mayonnaise, such as Hellmann's
Freshly ground black pepper

Melt 2 tablespoons of the butter in a medium (10-inch) sauté pan over medium heat. Add the scallions and corn and sauté for 3 minutes, until softened. Add the lobster and cook for 1 minute. Set aside.

Combine the flour, baking powder, paprika, Old Bay seasoning, and 1 teaspoon salt in a large mixing bowl. Make a well in the center and whisk in the eggs and half-and-half, stirring until the mixture is smooth, like a thick pancake batter. Stir in the corn and lobster mixture. (The batter may be made up to an hour ahead and refrigerated.)

For the sauce, place the garlic, saffron, sriracha, lemon juice, mayonnaise, ¼ teaspoon salt, and ¼ teaspoon pepper in the bowl of a food processor fitted with the steel blade and purée until smooth.

To make the fritters, heat 2 to 3 tablespoons of the butter in a large (12-inch) sauté pan over medium to medium-high heat. For each fritter, drop 2 rounded tablespoons of the batter into the hot butter and cook for 2 to 3 minutes on each side, until golden brown and firm to the touch. Don't crowd the skillet or they won't brown evenly. Repeat until all the batter is used, adding butter as necessary. Serve the fritters hot with a dollop of sauce on the side.

You can keep the fritters hot in a 300-degree oven while you cook the rest.

fennel & garlic shrimp

SERVES 2 TO 3

*This is a really simple first course to prepare. You can cook most of it in advance
and then just reheat the fennel, add the shrimp, and sauté it all together. I serve it
in bowls with lots of crusty bread to soak up all the garlicky juices.*

  6 tablespoons good olive oil
  1 cup chopped fennel bulb, fronds reserved
  3 tablespoons minced garlic (9 cloves)
  ¼ teaspoon crushed red pepper flakes
  1 pound (16- to 20-count) shrimp, peeled with tails on
  1 tablespoon chopped fresh flat-leaf parsley
  1 tablespoon Pernod (optional)
  1 teaspoon fleur de sel
  ½ teaspoon freshly ground black pepper
    French bread for serving

Heat the olive oil in a large (12-inch) sauté pan over medium heat.
Add the fennel and sauté for 5 minutes, until tender but not browned.
Turn the heat to medium-low, add the garlic and red pepper flakes,
and cook at a very low sizzle for 2 to 3 minutes, until the garlic just
begins to color.

Pat the shrimp dry with paper towels, add them to the pan, and toss
together with the fennel and olive oil. Spread the shrimp in one layer
and cook over medium heat for 2 minutes on one side. Turn the
shrimp and cook for 2 minutes on the other side, until they're pink
and just cooked through.

*To double this recipe,
you'll want to use
two 12-inch sauté pans
so the shrimp cook
properly.*

Off the heat, sprinkle with parsley, 1 tablespoon of chopped fennel
fronds, the Pernod (if using), the fleur de sel, and black pepper and
serve it with bread to soak up all the pan juices.

salmon & guacamole sandwiches

SERVES 4

The key to moist salmon is to undercook it and then allow it to rest under aluminum foil. While it rests, it will continue to cook and the juices will stay in the fish. This sandwich hits all the right notes—moist salmon, creamy guacamole, peppery arugula, and smoky crisp bacon on ciabatta bread.

8 slices applewood-smoked bacon (8 ounces)
2 ripe avocados, seeded and peeled
¼ cup freshly squeezed lime juice (2 limes)
4 scallions, white and green parts, chopped
¼ cup minced red onion
1 tablespoon jalapeño pepper, seeded and minced
1 teaspoon minced garlic
Kosher salt and freshly ground black pepper
Four (6-ounce) salmon fillets, skin on
Good olive oil
4 individual ciabatta rolls
Baby arugula leaves

You can prepare the bacon and guacamole in advance; cook the salmon and toast the ciabatta just before serving.

Preheat the oven to 400 degrees.

Place a baking rack on a sheet pan and lay the bacon on the rack. Roast for 15 to 20 minutes, until browned. Remove to a plate lined with paper towels.

Meanwhile, prepare the guacamole. Place the avocados, lime juice, scallions, red onion, jalapeño pepper, garlic, 1 teaspoon salt, and ½ teaspoon pepper in a mixing bowl and mash roughly together with a fork. Taste for seasoning; it should be very highly seasoned. Set aside.

When the bacon is done, heat a dry cast-iron skillet over high heat for 5 minutes. Pat the salmon fillets dry with paper towels, brush them all over—top and bottom—with olive oil, and sprinkle generously with salt and pepper. Place the fillets in the skillet skin side up and allow them to cook without disturbing them for 2 minutes exactly. With a metal spatula, carefully turn the fillets and cook for 2 more minutes. Transfer the skillet to the oven for 2 minutes (time it carefully!). Remove the salmon to a plate and cover it tightly with aluminum foil. Allow it to rest for 10 minutes.

While the salmon rests, cut the ciabatta rolls in half crosswise, place them cut side up on a sheet pan, and toast in the oven for 5 to 10 minutes, until lightly toasted. To assemble the sandwiches, place the bottoms of the ciabatta rolls on a board and spread each with 2 rounded tablespoons of guacamole. Remove the skin from the salmon fillets, cut each fillet in half crosswise, and place both halves on top of the guacamole. Add 2 slices of bacon, a handful of arugula, and a sprinkling of salt. Spread another rounded tablespoon of guacamole on the underside of the top bread and place on top. Continue arranging all the sandwiches. Cut each sandwich in half diagonally and serve warm or at room temperature.

lobster & potato salad

SERVES 6

The name Barefoot Contessa is about the juxtaposition of elegant and earthy. I've always loved that kind of food: pasta with caviar, mashed potatoes with truffles, and this lobster and potato salad with lemon-mustard vinaigrette. Make it a few hours in advance to allow the flavors to develop.

1½ pounds unpeeled small Yukon Gold potatoes (1½-inch diameter)
   Kosher salt
3 tablespoons Champagne or white wine vinegar
½ teaspoon Dijon mustard
½ teaspoon minced garlic
1 extra-large egg yolk, at room temperature (optional)
   Freshly ground black pepper
½ cup good olive oil
¼ cup dry white wine
3 tablespoons drained capers
1 cup thinly sliced scallions (6 to 8 scallions)
½ cup (¼-inch) diced celery
½ cup (¼-inch) diced red onion
1½ pounds cooked lobster meat, 1-inch-diced (see note)
1 lemon
3 tablespoons coarsely chopped fresh tarragon

If you're cooking them yourself, 4 to 5 (1-pound) lobsters will yield 1½ pounds of lobster meat.

Place the potatoes in a large pot and cover with water by 1 inch. Add 1 tablespoon salt and bring to a boil. Lower the heat and simmer for 15 to 25 minutes, depending on the size of the potatoes, until just tender. (I use a small bamboo skewer to test them.) Drain in a colander, cover the colander with a clean kitchen towel, and allow the potatoes to steam for 5 to 10 minutes. Cut them in quarters or halves, depending on their size, and place them in a large bowl.

Meanwhile, whisk together the vinegar, mustard, garlic, egg yolk, 2 teaspoons salt, and 1 teaspoon pepper. While whisking, slowly pour in the olive oil, making an emulsion. Stir in the wine and capers.

While the potatoes are still very warm, pour half the vinaigrette on the potatoes and toss them gently, allowing them to soak up the vinaigrette. Stir in the scallions, celery, red onion, and lobster and add enough vinaigrette to moisten. Reserve any remaining vinaigrette. Add the zest and juice of the lemon, the tarragon, 2 teaspoons salt, and 1 teaspoon pepper and toss carefully. Cover with plastic wrap and refrigerate for at least an hour to allow the flavors to blend. Taste for seasonings and add more vinaigrette, if necessary. Serve at room temperature.

israeli couscous
& tuna salad

SERVES 6 TO 8

This salad can be lunch on its own or part of a lunch buffet. The combination of couscous, which is a Middle Eastern pasta, plus tuna, olives, peppers, and lots of garlic and lemon is great for entertaining because it gets better as it sits. Israeli couscous has larger grains than regular couscous and absorbs all the flavors very well. I prefer the flavor and texture of Italian tuna that comes packed in olive oil.

2 cups Israeli couscous (10 to 12 ounces)

2 (7-ounce) cans or jars Italian tuna, drained and flaked

2 teaspoons grated lemon zest (2 lemons)

¼ cup freshly squeezed lemon juice

½ cup good olive oil

3 tablespoons capers, drained

½ cup pitted, oil-cured black olives, coarsely chopped (3 ounces)

½ cup jarred roasted red peppers, medium-diced (4 ounces)

2 teaspoons minced garlic (2 cloves)

　Kosher salt and freshly ground black pepper

1 cup chopped scallions (6 to 8 scallions)

¼ cup julienned fresh basil leaves, lightly packed

　Juice of ½ lemon

This can be made a day in advance. Bring back to room temperature and add the scallions, basil, and lemon juice before serving.

Bring 4 cups of water to a boil in a medium-size saucepan. Add the couscous and reduce the heat to very low. Cover the pot and simmer for 12 to 15 minutes, until the couscous is just tender. (I pull the pot halfway off the heat.) Drain in a colander.

Meanwhile, combine the tuna, lemon zest, lemon juice, olive oil, capers, olives, red peppers, garlic, 1 tablespoon salt, and 1½ teaspoons black pepper in a large bowl. Pour the hot couscous into the mixture and stir well. Cover and set aside for 10 to 15 minutes, stirring occasionally. Just before serving, stir in the scallions, basil, juice of the ½ lemon, and 1 more teaspoon of salt. Taste for seasonings and serve warm or at room temperature.

balsamic roasted beet salad

SERVES 6

Roasting beets takes some time in the oven but it's so little trouble and they're so much better than beets from a can. This salad has really great flavor and color with sweet beets, spicy arugula, salty almonds, and creamy goat cheese.

To toast the almonds, place them on a sheet pan and roast at 400 degrees for 10 minutes, turning once, until they are lightly browned. Sprinkle with salt and set aside.

8 medium-size beets, tops removed and scrubbed
½ cup balsamic vinegar
½ cup good olive oil
2 teaspoons Dijon mustard, such as Grey Poupon
Kosher salt and freshly ground black pepper
4 ounces baby arugula
⅓ cup roasted, salted Marcona almonds, toasted (see note)
4 ounces soft goat cheese, such as Montrachet, crumbled

Preheat the oven to 400 degrees.

Wrap the beets individually in aluminum foil and place them on a sheet pan. Roast them for 50 minutes to 1 hour, depending on their size, until a small sharp knife inserted in the middle indicates that they are tender. Unwrap each beet and set aside for 10 minutes, until cool enough to handle. Peel the beets with a small, sharp knife over a piece of parchment paper to prevent staining your cutting board.

Meanwhile, whisk together the vinegar, olive oil, mustard, 2 teaspoons salt, and 1 teaspoon pepper and set aside. While the beets are still warm, cut each one in half and then each half into 4 to 6 wedges and place them in a large mixing bowl. As you're cutting the beets, toss them with half of the vinaigrette (warm beets absorb more vinaigrette), 1 teaspoon salt, and ¼ teaspoon pepper. Taste for seasonings.

Place the arugula in a separate bowl and toss it with enough vinaigrette to moisten. Put the arugula on a serving platter and then arrange the beets, almonds, and goat cheese on top. Drizzle with additional vinaigrette, if desired, sprinkle with salt and pepper, and serve warm or at room temperature.

roasted asparagus & prosciutto

SERVES 3

This is a great lunch—roasted fresh asparagus, crisp prosciutto, soft runny egg, and a drizzle of lemony hollandaise. Peel the asparagus in advance and keep them in the fridge.

> 1 **pound fresh asparagus (not too thin)**
> **Good olive oil**
> **Kosher salt and freshly ground black pepper**
> 6 **large slices prosciutto**
> 1½ **tablespoons unsalted butter**
> 3 **extra-large eggs**
> **Easy Hollandaise Sauce (recipe follows)**

Preheat the oven to 400 degrees.

If the asparagus are thick, peel them halfway up the stalks. Cut off and discard the bottom third of the asparagus. Place the asparagus in a single layer on a sheet pan, drizzle with olive oil, and sprinkle with 1 teaspoon salt and ½ teaspoon pepper. Roast for 10 minutes, until the stalks are just tender. Meanwhile, place the prosciutto in a single layer on another sheet pan and roast in the same oven for 5 minutes.

Melt the butter in a medium (10-inch) sauté pan over medium heat and wait until the bubbles almost subside. Crack the eggs into the skillet, keeping them separate, if possible. Sprinkle the eggs generously with salt and pepper and cook over medium heat until the whites are cooked but the yolks are still runny. Don't turn them over!

Arrange the asparagus on 3 plates. Place 2 slices of prosciutto on top of each pile, drizzle with hollandaise, and place a fried egg on top of the prosciutto. Serve hot.

easy hollandaise sauce

MAKES ½ CUP

2 extra-large egg yolks, at room temperature
1½ tablespoons freshly squeezed lemon juice
¾ teaspoon kosher salt
¼ teaspoon freshly ground black pepper
Pinch of cayenne pepper
6 tablespoons (¾ stick) unsalted butter

Place the egg yolks, lemon juice, salt, black pepper, and cayenne pepper in the jar of a blender and process on low for 15 seconds. Melt the butter in a small saucepan until it is sizzling hot. Remove the small clear insert in the top of the blender. With the blender on low, slowly add the hot butter to the egg and lemon mixture and blend for 30 seconds, until the sauce is very thick. Use immediately.

You can make the hollandaise up to an hour in advance and leave it at room temperature. Before serving, add a tablespoon of very hot tap water and blend again.

white bean & arugula salad

SERVES 6

I used to make a salad like this at Barefoot Contessa but when I revisited my old recipe, I found it a little boring. The addition of sun-dried tomatoes, garlic, rosemary, prosciutto, and freshly squeezed lemon juice made it more flavorful. I fill a shallow serving bowl with the white beans and make a wreath of peppery arugula around it.

- ¾ pound dried cannellini beans
- 2 tablespoons plus ½ cup good olive oil
- 1 red onion, halved lengthwise and sliced into ¼-inch-thick half-rounds
- 2 ounces sun-dried tomatoes in oil, drained and small-diced
- 4 teaspoons minced garlic (4 cloves)
- 2 teaspoons minced fresh rosemary leaves
- ¼ teaspoon crushed red pepper flakes
- 2 ounces thinly sliced prosciutto, small-diced
- 1 teaspoon grated lemon zest
- ¼ cup freshly squeezed lemon juice (2 lemons)
- Kosher salt and freshly ground black pepper
- 2 ounces baby arugula

The night before, place the beans in a large bowl and add water to cover by 2 inches. Soak overnight in the refrigerator. The following day, drain the beans, rinse under cold water, and drain again.

Heat the 2 tablespoons of olive oil in a large, heavy-bottomed pot over medium heat. Add the red onion and sauté over medium-low heat for 7 to 9 minutes, until wilted. Add the beans and enough water to cover them by 3 inches. Bring to a boil and skim off any foam that rises to the surface. Reduce the heat and simmer gently for 45 minutes, until tender. Drain the beans and onions and transfer to a mixing bowl.

Meanwhile, heat the ½ cup of olive oil in a 10- to 12-inch sauté pan over medium-high heat. Add the sun-dried tomatoes, garlic, rosemary, red pepper flakes, and prosciutto and cook for 4 to 5 minutes, until fragrant. Pour the hot oil mixture over the warm drained beans, tossing well. Allow to cool for 10 minutes only. While still warm, stir in the lemon zest, lemon juice, 2 teaspoons salt, and 1 teaspoon black pepper. Place in a large, shallow serving bowl, surround with arugula, taste for seasonings, and serve warm or at room temperature.

dinner

crispy mustard-roasted chicken

chicken with wild mushrooms

accidental turkey

slow-roasted filet of beef with basil
parmesan mayonnaise

mustard-marinated flank steak

1770 house meatloaf

veal chops with
caramelized shallots

lamb shanks & orzo

roasted sausages & grapes

four-hour lamb with french
flageolets

foolproof ribs with barbecue sauce

osso buco

seared scallops &
potato celery root purée

sicilian grilled swordfish

salmon & melting
cherry tomatoes

orecchiette with broccoli rabe
& sausage

lobster mac & cheese

straw & hay with gorgonzola

penne alla vecchia bettola

amelia's jambalaya

can i freeze it?

By far, this is the question I get asked the most. Can I grill fish for twenty people, freeze it, and serve it next week? Can I bake cookies in October and freeze them to serve at Christmas? What's the best way to defrost a cake? Can I freeze mashed potatoes? I don't think there's a recipe I've written that someone hasn't wanted to make ahead and freeze.

If you look in my freezer, you can probably figure out how little I freeze prepared food. You'll see vodka, chicken stock, puff pastry, truffle butter, vanilla ice cream, and maybe some leftover bread (for bread crumbs) but that's about it. Long ago, I realized that prepared food tends to go into my freezer and it almost never comes out because I'd rather eat something fresh than frozen, but I often use frozen ingredients. There are nights, though, that I truly don't have time to cook and on those occasions I think how wonderful it would be to have a freezer filled with delicious things to heat and serve. The freezer is a really good tool for making things easy. And for anyone who wants to avoid lots of processed foods but has little time to cook during the week, making food ahead and freezing it is a necessity. Fortunately, there are all kinds of soups, sauces, baked dinners, vegetables, and baked desserts that freeze beautifully. Here are some of my guidelines:

1. Soups generally freeze very well unless they have cheese or milk in them. (The milk can curdle when the soup's reheated.) Vegetable soups, chicken soups, creamed soups—they'll all be perfect when they're defrosted and reheated.

2. Don't freeze any raw food that's already been frozen once, such as shrimp or chicken. Remember, raw shrimp from the seafood shop has probably been frozen and thawed before you bought it. Once it's cooked, you can refreeze it, but again, just once.

3. Dishes that contain sauces, such as stews, and baked pastas freeze better than simply cooked dishes like roast chicken and filet of beef, which are more likely to suffer in the process.

4. Steamed or sautéed vegetables need to be flash frozen individually, which is hard to do at home, but cooked vegetable gratins will be more likely to survive in good shape.

5. If you want a dish you can make ahead and freeze, your best bet is to make a sauce like marinara or pesto. Defrost it, cook some pasta, toss on the sauce, and you have a fresh dinner ready in 10 minutes!

6. The best way to defrost anything is slowly overnight in the refrigerator rather than leaving it at room temperature or defrosting it in the microwave.

7. Baked goods usually freeze well but not icings or glazes. If I need to freeze a cake, I would bake it, cool it completely, wrap it well, then make the icing or glaze the day of the party.

8. Freeze cookie dough rather than the baked cookies. Defrost the dough, and then bake the cookies as usual.

9. Air is the enemy of freezing—that's when "freezer burn" happens. Wrap anything you're freezing as tightly as possible in plastic wrap, vacuum seal it, or seal it with freezer tape. You can place most things in a Ziploc bag and press the bag around the food to remove as much air as possible.

10. Write the date on *everything* with an indelible marker. Nothing survives forever and you'll want to know if you made that chicken soup last month or ten years ago before you serve it. Once or twice a year, go through the freezer and use or toss anything that's gotten a little long in the tooth.

crispy mustard-roasted chicken

SERVES 3

I'm always looking for an easy chicken dish. For this, whisk together Dijon mustard and white wine and use it as a coating for chicken the way you'd use beaten eggs, then dip it in flavorful panko crumbs. Moist and crispy chicken every time!

- 4 garlic cloves
- 1 tablespoon minced fresh thyme leaves
  Kosher salt and freshly ground black pepper
- 2 cups panko (Japanese bread flakes)
- 1 tablespoon grated lemon zest (2 lemons)
- 2 tablespoons good olive oil
- 2 tablespoons unsalted butter, melted
- ½ cup Dijon mustard, such as Grey Poupon
- ½ cup dry white wine
- 1 (3½- to 4-pound) chicken, cut in eighths

Preheat the oven to 350 degrees.

To make in advance, prepare the chicken without baking it. Refrigerate and then bake before dinner.

Place the garlic, thyme, 2 teaspoons salt, and 1 teaspoon pepper in a food processor fitted with the steel blade and process until the garlic is finely minced. Add the panko, lemon zest, olive oil, and butter and pulse a few times to moisten the bread flakes. Pour the mixture onto a large plate. In a shallow bowl, whisk together the mustard and wine.

Pat the chicken dry with paper towels. Sprinkle generously all over with salt and pepper. Dip each piece in the mustard mixture to coat on all sides, and then place skin-side down *only* into the crumb mixture, pressing gently to make the crumbs adhere. Place the chicken on a sheet pan crumb-side up. Press the remaining crumbs on the chicken pieces.

Bake the chicken for 40 minutes. Raise the heat to 400 degrees and bake for another 10 minutes, until the crumbs are browned and the chicken is cooked through. Serve hot, warm, or at room temperature.

chicken
with wild mushrooms

SERVES 6

Chicken and mushrooms can be boring, but simmered on top of the stove with lots of garlic, sherry, and thyme, they can be delicious. I like this recipe because you can assemble it in advance and then just throw it in the oven before dinner. It creates its own savory sauce, which is wonderful spooned over couscous.

Don't flour the chicken in advance; you want the skin to be dry so it browns.

To make in advance, prepare the dish completely, allow to cool, and refrigerate the chicken in the sauce with the lid on the pot. To serve, reheat slowly over low heat until the chicken is heated through.

2	(3½- to 4-pound) chickens, cut in eighths
	Kosher salt and freshly ground black pepper
	All-purpose flour
½	cup good olive oil
8	whole garlic cloves
1½	pounds assorted wild mushrooms, such as porcini and cremini, stems removed and (1½-inch) diced
8	sprigs fresh thyme, tied with kitchen string
¼	cup dry sherry
1	tablespoon minced garlic (3 cloves)
2	cups white wine, such as Pinot Grigio
2	cups good chicken stock, preferably homemade (page 62)
3	tablespoons unsalted butter, at room temperature

Preheat the oven to 325 degrees.

Pat the chicken dry with paper towels and sprinkle both sides liberally with salt and pepper. Place ½ cup flour in a bowl and dredge the chicken in the flour. In a large (12-inch) ovenproof pot such as Le Creuset, heat the oil. Add the chicken in three batches (don't crowd them!) and brown lightly over medium-high heat for 3 to 5 minutes on each side. Remove the chicken to a plate and continue until all the chicken is browned.

Add the whole garlic cloves, mushrooms, and thyme to the pot and cook over medium heat for 5 minutes, stirring occasionally. Add the sherry and cook for 1 minute, scraping up the brown bits. Add the minced garlic and cook for 2 more minutes. Add the wine, chicken stock, 1 tablespoon salt, and 1 teaspoon pepper and bring to a simmer. Add the chicken (large pieces first), cover, and place in the middle of the oven for 30 to 35 minutes, until the chicken is cooked through (about 165 degrees on an instant-read thermometer).

Remove the chicken to a bowl and discard the thyme. With a fork, mash together the butter and ¼ cup flour and add it to the sauce. Simmer, stirring constantly, over medium heat for 5 minutes, until slightly thickened. Season to taste (it should be highly seasoned), put the chicken back in the sauce, and serve hot.

accidental turkey

SERVES 10

Everyone has a turkey disaster story, but this one actually had a happy ending. My friend Pam Krauss once put her turkey in the oven at 450 degrees and forgot to turn the temperature down after 10 minutes, which is how she usually roasts a turkey. When the kitchen filled with smoke after an hour, she thought she'd ruined dinner. Instead of burnt turkey, she found it was the moistest and most delicious one she'd ever made! The dry brine also makes this the most flavorful turkey I've ever eaten.

> Kosher salt
> 1 tablespoon minced fresh rosemary leaves
> Grated zest of 1 lemon
> 1 (12- to 14-pound) fresh turkey
> 1 large yellow onion, unpeeled and cut in eighths
> 1 lemon, quartered
> 8 sprigs fresh thyme
> 4 tablespoons (½ stick) unsalted butter, melted
> Freshly ground black pepper

Two or three days before you plan to roast the turkey, combine 3 tablespoons salt, the rosemary, and lemon zest. Wash the turkey inside and out, drain it well, and pat it dry with paper towels. Sprinkle 1 tablespoon of the salt mixture in the cavity of the turkey and rub the rest on the skin, including under the wings and legs. Place the turkey in a shallow dish to catch any drips and wrap the whole dish tightly with plastic wrap. Refrigerate for one or two days. The day before you plan to roast the turkey, remove the plastic wrap and leave it in the fridge. The skin will dry out and turn a little translucent.

Preheat the oven to 450 degrees. Be sure your oven is *very* clean!

Place the onion, lemon, and thyme in the cavity. Tie the legs together with kitchen string and tie the wings close to the body. Brush the turkey with the butter and sprinkle it with salt and pepper.

Roast the turkey for 45 minutes, placing it in the oven legs first. Lower the temperature to 325 degrees and roast it for about another hour, until 165 degrees for the breast and 180 degrees in the thigh on an instant-read thermometer. Remove from the oven, cover the turkey tightly with aluminum foil, and allow it to rest for 20 to 30 minutes. Carve and serve with the pan juices.

slow-roasted filet of beef
with basil parmesan mayonnaise

SERVES 6 TO 8

I had always cooked filet of beef at a high temperature to sear the outside and keep the inside moist and rare. Recently, though, I tried slow-roasting a filet of beef, and found it was the tenderest I'd ever tasted. Prep it in advance and throw it in the oven two hours before dinner. The homemade mayonnaise with basil and Parmesan is a delicious accompaniment.

1	whole filet of beef tenderloin, trimmed and tied (4½ pounds)
3	tablespoons good olive oil
4	teaspoons kosher salt
2	teaspoons coarsely ground black pepper
10 to 15	branches fresh tarragon
	Basil Parmesan Mayonnaise, for serving (recipe follows)

Preheat the oven to 275 degrees. Use an oven thermometer to be sure your oven temperature is accurate!

Place the filet on a sheet pan and pat it dry with paper towels. Brush the filet all over with the oil, reserving about half a tablespoon. Sprinkle it all over with the salt and pepper (it will seem like a lot but believe me, it makes a difference). Place the tarragon branches around the beef, tying them in 4 or 5 places with kitchen string to keep them in place, and then brush the tarragon with the reserved oil.

Roast the filet of beef for 1¼ to 1½ hours, until the temperature registers 125 degrees in the center for rare and 135 degrees for medium-rare. I place the thermometer horizontally through the end of the beef. Cover the filet with aluminum foil and allow to rest for 20 minutes. Slice thickly and serve warm or at room temperature with Basil Parmesan Mayonnaise.

basil parmesan mayonnaise

MAKES ABOUT 2 CUPS

Homemade mayonnaise sounds intimidating but there's really only one trick: the eggs and oil must be totally at room temperature. Adding fresh basil leaves and salty Parmesan cheese makes this a great sauce for filet of beef but it's also delicious as a sandwich spread, a dip for crudités, or served with a flavorful fish like salmon or swordfish.

  2 **extra-large egg yolks, at room temperature**

  3 **tablespoons freshly squeezed lemon juice**

  ½ **cup freshly grated Parmesan cheese (see note)**

  1 **tablespoon Dijon mustard**

  ½ **cup chopped fresh basil leaves, lightly packed**

  ½ **teaspoon minced garlic**

      Kosher salt and freshly ground black pepper

  1 **cup vegetable oil, at room temperature**

  ½ **cup good olive oil, at room temperature**

I "grate" the Parmesan in the food processor—it's actually ground, which is better than grated.

Place the egg yolks, lemon juice, Parmesan, mustard, basil, garlic, 1 tablespoon salt, and 1 teaspoon pepper in a food processor fitted with the steel blade. Process for 20 seconds, until smooth. Combine the vegetable oil and olive oil in a 2-cup liquid measuring cup. With the processor running, slowly pour the oil mixture through the feed tube to make a thick emulsion. Taste for seasonings—the mayonnaise is a sauce so it should be highly seasoned. Store in the refrigerator until ready to use; it will keep for up to a week.

mustard-marinated flank steak

SERVES 4 TO 5

My wonderful assistant Barbara asked me to come up with a flank steak recipe for her. I'm so glad I did! It's flavored with lots of mustard, shallots, garlic, and fresh tarragon and is so easy to prepare. You can marinate the steak up to a day in advance and grill it just before dinner.

1 flank steak (2 to 2½ pounds)
⅓ cup dry white wine
⅓ cup good olive oil
⅓ cup Dijon mustard
Kosher salt and freshly ground black pepper
⅓ cup chopped shallots (2 shallots)
1 tablespoon minced garlic (3 cloves)
2 tablespoons coarsely chopped fresh tarragon leaves

Fresh tarragon is widely available and has a delicate anise flavor.

Place the steak flat in a large nonreactive dish such as glass or porcelain. Using the tip of a sharp knife, lightly score the top of the steak diagonally in a large crisscross pattern to make what looks like 1-inch diamonds across the steak. This allows the marinade to penetrate into the meat.

In a 2-cup measuring cup, whisk together the wine, olive oil, mustard, 1 teaspoon salt, and ½ teaspoon pepper. Stir in the shallots and garlic. Pour the marinade over and under the steak until it's completely coated. Scatter the tarragon on top. Cover the dish with plastic wrap and allow it to marinate in the refrigerator for at least 2 hours but preferably overnight.

Half an hour before serving, remove the steak from the refrigerator and heat a charcoal grill with a layer of hot coals. (You can also set a gas grill on medium-high heat.) Sprinkle the steak with 1 teaspoon salt and 1 teaspoon pepper. Discard the remaining marinade.

Grill the steak for about 5 minutes per side for medium-rare. Place the steak on a clean plate, cover tightly with aluminum foil, and allow to rest for 10 minutes. Slice the steak thin, cutting diagonally across the grain. Sprinkle with salt and serve hot.

1770 house meatloaf

SERVES 6 TO 8

The 1770 House is a restaurant in East Hampton where I could eat dinner every night. The executive chef is Kevin Penner and he makes delicious "home-style" food that's both elegant and comforting. I'm embarrassed to say how many winter nights we've ordered this amazing meatloaf with sweet roasted garlic sauce. The secret, as they say, is in the sauce.

2	tablespoons good olive oil
2	cups chopped Spanish onion (1 large)
1½	cups small-diced celery (2 stalks)
1	pound ground beef
1	pound ground veal
1	pound ground pork
1	tablespoon chopped fresh flat-leaf parsley
1	tablespoon chopped fresh thyme leaves
1	tablespoon chopped fresh chives
3	extra-large eggs, lightly beaten
⅔	cup whole milk
2	tablespoons kosher salt
1	tablespoon freshly ground black pepper
2½	cups panko (Japanese bread flakes)
	Garlic Sauce (recipe follows)

Preheat the oven to 350 degrees.

Heat the olive oil in a large (12-inch) sauté pan over medium heat. Add the onion and celery and cook for 5 to 7 minutes, stirring occasionally, until the onion is translucent but not browned. Set aside to cool slightly.

Place the beef, veal, pork, parsley, thyme, chives, eggs, milk, salt, and pepper in a large mixing bowl. Put the panko in a food processor fitted with the steel blade and process until the panko is finely ground.

Add the onion mixture and the panko to the meat mixture. With clean hands, gently toss the mixture together, making sure it's combined but not compacted.

Place a piece of parchment paper on a sheet pan. Pat the meat into a flat rectangle and then press the sides in until it forms a cylinder down the middle of the pan (this will ensure no air pockets). Bake for 40 to 50 minutes, until a thermometer inserted in the middle reads 155 to 160 degrees. Remove from the oven and allow to rest for 10 minutes. Slice and serve hot with the Garlic Sauce.

garlic sauce

Choose firm heads of garlic that have no green sprouts.

¾ cup good olive oil
10 garlic cloves, peeled
2 cups chicken stock, preferably homemade (page 62)
3 tablespoons unsalted butter, at room temperature
Kosher salt and freshly ground black pepper

Combine the oil and garlic in a small saucepan and bring to a boil. Lower the heat and simmer for 10 to 15 minutes, until lightly browned. Be careful not to burn the garlic or it will be bitter. Remove the garlic from the oil and set aside. (I save the oil for vinaigrettes.)

Combine the chicken stock, butter, and cooked garlic in a medium saucepan and bring to a boil. Lower the heat and cook at a full boil for 35 to 40 minutes, until slightly thickened. Mash the garlic with a fork, whisk in ½ teaspoon salt and ¼ teaspoon pepper, and taste for seasonings. Spoon the warm sauce over the meatloaf.

veal chops
with caramelized shallots

SERVES 4

I've tried to get this dish right for years and I've finally perfected it. The roasted shallots and garlic are the perfect accompaniment to juicy grilled veal chops. Be sure all the chops are the same thickness so they cook evenly.

15 whole shallots, trimmed with the root ends intact
24 whole garlic cloves (2 heads)
4 tablespoons (½ stick) unsalted butter, divided
   Kosher salt and freshly ground black pepper
⅓ cup good sherry vinegar
½ cup ruby port wine
1½ tablespoons light brown sugar
1 teaspoon fresh thyme leaves, plus sprigs for serving
4 (10- to 14-ounce) bone-in rib veal chops, 1 to 1½ inches thick
3 tablespoons good olive oil, plus extra for grilling

Preheat the oven to 375 degrees.

Bring a medium pot of water to a boil and add the shallots and garlic for 15 seconds. Drain and peel them; blanching makes peeling easy. If any shallots are very large, cut them in half through the root so they stay intact.

In a large (12-inch) ovenproof sauté pan, melt 2 tablespoons of the butter, add the shallots, garlic, 1 teaspoon salt, and ½ teaspoon pepper, and sauté for 2 minutes over medium-high heat. Place the pan in the oven for 30 minutes, tossing once, until the shallots and garlic are lightly browned.

Place the pan on the stovetop, add the remaining 2 tablespoons of butter, and sauté over medium heat for 3 minutes. Add the vinegar and port, bring to a boil, lower the heat, and simmer for 6 minutes, until the liquid is reduced. Add the brown sugar and thyme and cook for 1 minute, until syrupy.

Meanwhile, place the veal chops on a board and pat them dry. Rub all over with olive oil and sprinkle generously on both sides with salt and pepper. Set aside for 30 minutes while you prepare a charcoal fire or heat a gas grill to medium heat. If you're using charcoal, make only one or two layers of hot coals.

Grill the veal chops for 6 to 8 minutes per side, until nicely browned and cooked to an internal temperature of 145 degrees. Transfer to a serving platter, cover tightly with foil, and allow to rest for 10 minutes. Reheat the shallots and garlic and spoon over the veal chops, sprinkle with extra thyme and salt, and serve hot.

lamb shanks & orzo

SERVES 4

On a cold winter night, braised lamb shanks are the most satisfying meal.
They're particularly great for a party because you throw them in the oven and
forget about them until you're ready to serve dinner. The rich sauce made with
tomatoes, onions, garlic, and rosemary gets absorbed into the orzo that you cook
in the same pot.

Grapeseed oil has a high burning point so you can sear the lamb shanks over high heat without scorching.

1 cup all-purpose flour
  Kosher salt and freshly ground black pepper
4 lamb shanks (1 to 1½ pounds each)
  Grapeseed oil
2 tablespoons good olive oil
3 cups chopped yellow onions (2 to 3 onions)
2 cups medium-diced carrots (4 to 5 carrots)
2 cups medium-diced celery (3 stalks)
1 tablespoon minced fresh rosemary leaves
3 large garlic cloves, minced
2 (14.5-ounce) cans diced tomatoes, including the liquid
2 cups canned beef broth
1½ cups dry white wine, plus extra for serving
2 bay leaves
2 cups orzo

Preheat the oven to 325 degrees.

Combine the flour, 2 teaspoons salt, and 1 teaspoon pepper in a bowl
and dredge the lamb shanks in the mixture, shaking off the excess.
In a large (13-inch) Dutch oven such as Le Creuset, heat 3 tablespoons
of the grapeseed oil over medium-high heat. Add 2 lamb shanks and
cook for 10 minutes, turning every few minutes, until browned on
all sides. Transfer the shanks to a plate, add more grapeseed oil, and
brown the remaining 2 shanks.

Wipe out the Dutch oven with a paper towel, add the olive oil, and heat
over medium to medium-high heat. Add the onions, carrots, celery, and

rosemary and cook for 8 to 10 minutes, until the vegetables are tender. Add the garlic and cook 1 more minute. Add the tomatoes, beef broth, wine, 4 teaspoons salt, and 2 teaspoons pepper. Add the lamb shanks, arranging them so they're almost completely submerged in the liquid. Tuck in the bay leaves and bring to a simmer on top of the stove. Cover the pot and place it in the oven for 2 hours, turning the shanks once while they cook.

Stir in the orzo and return the lamb shanks to the oven for 20 to 30 minutes, until the orzo is cooked and the lamb shanks are very tender. Discard the bay leaves, stir in 2 to 3 tablespoons of white wine, and taste the orzo for seasonings. Serve hot.

roasted sausages & grapes

One of my favorite restaurants in the world is Al Forno in Providence, Rhode Island. My friends George Germon and Johanne Killeen are famous for their baked pastas and grilled pizzas—and for thirty-one years they have had this dish on the menu. It's stunningly easy to make and such a satisfying winter meal. The spicy sausages and sweet roasted grapes are amazing served with a puddle of rich, creamy polenta or Truffled Mashed Potatoes (page 187).

1½ pounds sweet Italian pork sausages

1½ pounds hot Italian pork sausages

3 tablespoons unsalted butter

2½ pounds seedless green grapes, removed from the stems

½ cup good balsamic vinegar

Preheat the oven to 500 degrees.

Bring a large pot of water to a boil, add the sausages, and simmer for 8 minutes to remove some of the fat. Remove to a plate.

Melt the butter in a large (12 × 15-inch) roasting pan on top of the stove. Add the grapes and toss them to coat with butter. Transfer the sausages to the roasting pan with tongs, nestling them down in the grapes in one layer. Place in the oven and roast for 20 to 25 minutes, turning the sausages once, until they're browned and the grapes are tender.

Transfer the sausages and grapes to a serving platter with tongs and a slotted spoon and cover with aluminum foil to keep them hot. Add the balsamic vinegar to the roasting pan and cook over medium-high heat for 2 minutes to reduce the balsamic vinegar slightly. Pour over the sausages and grapes and serve hot.

four-hour lamb
with french flageolets

SERVES 6

At a very elegant wedding in Provence, my friend Barbara Liberman was served the earthiest French dinner—gigot de sept heures, or seven-hour lamb. When I made it, I realized that after four hours the lamb was tender, delicious, and falling off the bone, so I stopped cooking it. The lamb is flavored with garlic, rosemary, and white wine and is served with French beans called flageolets.

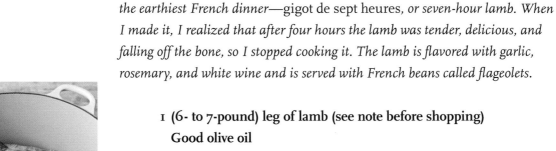

1 (6- to 7-pound) leg of lamb (see note before shopping)
   Good olive oil
   Kosher salt and freshly ground black pepper
1 (750-ml) bottle dry white wine
2 heads garlic, broken into cloves but not peeled
15 large sprigs fresh rosemary
15 large sprigs fresh thyme
6 bay leaves
   French Flageolet Beans (page 192)

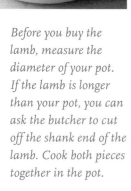

Before you buy the lamb, measure the diameter of your pot. If the lamb is longer than your pot, you can ask the butcher to cut off the shank end of the lamb. Cook both pieces together in the pot.

You can cook the lamb either tied or untied. If it's tied, discard the string before serving.

Preheat the oven to 300 degrees.

Rub the lamb all over with olive oil and season generously all over with 1 tablespoon salt and 2 teaspoons pepper. Heat a very large Dutch oven such as Le Creuset over medium-high heat until it's very hot. Add the lamb and sear on all sides for about 12 minutes, until it's evenly browned. Remove the lamb to a plate.

Add the wine and 2 cups of water to the pan and cook for 1 to 2 minutes, scraping up all the brown bits in the pan. Add the garlic, rosemary, thyme, and bay leaves and place the lamb on top. Put the lid on the pot and place it in the oven for 4 hours, basting occasionally. (If you don't have a lid, you can cover the pan tightly with 2 layers of aluminum foil.)

Test the lamb with a fork; it should be incredibly tender and falling off the bone. Remove the lamb to a plate, cover it tightly with foil, and allow it to rest. Strain the sauce into a saucepan, pressing the garlic solids through the strainer. Bring it to a boil, lower the heat, and simmer for 10 minutes, until reduced slightly. Taste for seasonings. The lamb will be too tender to slice; sprinkle it with salt and serve it whole with two large spoons with the flageolets and the sauce on the side.

foolproof ribs
with barbecue sauce

SERVES 6

The key to these amazing ribs—which couldn't be easier!—is that I bake (not barbecue) them in advance until they're very tender and almost falling off the bone. Then, before dinner, I grill them quickly to get all that good smoky flavor without burning them to a crisp. I make lots of extra sauce for dipping.

> 5 **pounds Danish baby back ribs (4 racks) or St. Louis ribs (2 racks)**
> **Kosher salt and freshly ground black pepper**
> 1 **recipe BC Barbecue Sauce (recipe follows)**

Preheat the oven to 350 degrees. Line a sheet pan with aluminum foil.

Place the ribs on the sheet pan meat side up and sprinkle them with 2 teaspoons salt and 1 teaspoon pepper. Pour the barbecue sauce generously on each rack and cover the ribs loosely with aluminum foil. Bake for 1½ hours for baby backs and 1¾ hours for St. Louis ribs, until the meat is very tender when tested with a fork. As soon as the ribs are out of the oven, spread them generously with additional barbecue sauce. Grill right away or refrigerate to grill later.

About 40 minutes before you want to serve, heat a charcoal grill with a layer of hot coals or heat a gas grill to medium-high heat. After the charcoal turns gray, brush the cooking grate with oil to keep the ribs from sticking. Place the ribs on the grill ribs-side-down, put the lid on top (be sure both vents are open!), and grill for 5 minutes. Turn the ribs meat-side-down, put the lid back on, and grill for another 4 to 5 minutes, until nicely browned. Place on a cutting board, cover tightly with aluminum foil, and allow the ribs to rest for 10 minutes. Cut into ribs and serve hot with extra barbecue sauce on the side.

bc barbecue sauce

MAKES 1½ QUARTS

This is a classic Barefoot Contessa recipe. It has a lot of ingredients, but it's easy to make and lasts for weeks in the refrigerator.

½ cup vegetable oil

1½ cups chopped yellow onion (1 large onion)

1 tablespoon minced garlic (3 cloves)

1 cup (10 ounces) tomato paste

1 cup cider vinegar

1 cup honey

½ cup Worcestershire sauce

1 cup Dijon mustard

½ cup soy sauce

1 cup hoisin sauce

2 tablespoons chili powder

1 tablespoon ground cumin

1½ teaspoons crushed red pepper flakes

Heat the oil in a large saucepan over low heat, add the onions, and cook for 10 to 15 minutes, until the onions are translucent but not browned. Add the garlic and cook for 1 more minute. Add the tomato paste, vinegar, honey, Worcestershire sauce, mustard, soy sauce, hoisin sauce, chili powder, cumin, and red pepper flakes. Bring to a boil, then lower the heat and simmer uncovered for 30 minutes. Use the sauce immediately or pour into a container and refrigerate.

osso buco

SERVES 6

*This is another terrific dish for entertaining on a cold winter night. I assemble
it in advance through the point where I return the shanks to the pot and then
refrigerate the whole pot. Two hours before dinner, I'll put it on the stove, bring
the liquid to a simmer, cover the pot, and throw it in the oven. I love this with any
kind of mashed potatoes to soak up all the delicious sauce.*

  8 large pieces of veal shank cut 2 inches thick, tied
1½ cups all-purpose flour
    Kosher salt and freshly ground black pepper
    Good olive oil
  3 tablespoons unsalted butter
  3 medium celery stalks, medium-diced
  2 carrots, medium-diced
  2 leeks, cleaned and medium-diced
  1 medium yellow onion, medium-diced
  4 teaspoons minced garlic (4 cloves)
  1 tablespoon grated lemon zest (2 lemons)
  5 sprigs fresh thyme, tied together with kitchen string
  1 cup dry white wine
  3 cups good chicken stock, preferably homemade (page 62)

Preheat the oven to 350 degrees.

Rinse the veal shanks and pat them dry. In a medium bowl, combine
the flour with 1 tablespoon salt and 1½ teaspoons pepper. Toss the veal
shanks in the flour and shake off any excess. In a pot or Dutch oven
large enough to hold the veal shanks in one layer, heat 2 tablespoons
of olive oil over high heat. In two batches, brown the veal shanks on
all sides for about 10 minutes, turning to brown evenly, and place
them on a plate. Add more oil, if necessary, to cook the second batch.

Wipe out the pot with a paper towel. Melt the butter in the pot, add
the celery, carrots, leeks, and onion, and sauté over medium heat for
10 minutes, until tender. Add the garlic and lemon zest and cook for

1 more minute. Add the thyme, wine, chicken stock, 1 tablespoon salt, and 1½ teaspoons pepper, scraping the pot to incorporate any browned bits. Return the shanks to the pot and bring the liquid to a simmer.

Cover the pot tightly and place in the oven for 1¾ to 2 hours, until the veal shanks are very tender. Taste for seasonings and serve the shanks hot with the sauce.

seared scallops
& potato celery root purée

SERVES 6

This is my favorite way to serve scallops—on a bed of potato and celery root purée. I make the purée before guests arrive and keep it warm over a double boiler. Before dinner, all I have to do is sear the scallops. For New Year's Eve I splurged and added shaved white truffles on top. That was worth celebrating!

If you don't have two 12-inch sauté pans, cook the scallops in batches and keep the first batch warm in a 250-degree oven until the second batch is ready.

Scallops are packed either wet or dry. Wet ones last longer but they won't sear; buy "dry" ones for this recipe.

5 tablespoons unsalted butter
6 cups chopped leeks, white and light green parts (4 leeks)
4 cups (¾-inch) diced peeled Yukon Gold potatoes (1½ pounds)
4 cups (¾-inch) diced peeled celery root (2 pounds)
3 cups heavy cream
 Kosher salt and freshly ground black pepper
24 to 26 large "dry" sea scallops (see note)
4 tablespoons grapeseed oil, divided
 Basil-infused olive oil, for serving
 Minced fresh chives, for serving

Melt the butter over medium heat in a large (8- to 10-inch) saucepan or Dutch oven. Rinse the leeks well in a colander, spin them dry in a salad spinner, and add them to the pot. Sauté them over medium-low heat, stirring occasionally, for 8 to 10 minutes, until tender but not browned. Add the potatoes, celery root, cream, 4 teaspoons salt, and 2 teaspoons pepper to the pot, stir, and bring to a boil. Lower the heat to very low, cover the pot, and simmer gently for 25 to 30 minutes, stirring occasionally, until the vegetables are tender. Be careful—don't let the vegetables scorch on the bottom of the pan! In batches, pour the mixture into the bowl of a food processor fitted with the steel blade and pulse until coarsely puréed. Taste for seasonings, return to the saucepan, and keep warm over very low heat. If the mixture gets too thick, add a little more cream.

If it hasn't already been removed, peel off the tough strip of muscle on the side of each scallop. Pat the scallops dry with paper towels and season them generously on both sides with salt and pepper. Heat two 12-inch sauté pans over medium-high heat. Add 2 tablespoons of grapeseed oil to each pan and, when the oil is almost smoking hot, add half the scallops to each pan. Cook undisturbed for about 3 minutes, until golden brown on the bottoms. Don't crowd the scallops or they'll steam rather than sear. Using a small metal spatula, turn the scallops and cook for 2 to 3 minutes more, until just cooked through. (If the pan is hot enough and you let the scallops cook undisturbed, they won't stick to the pan.)

Spoon the warm purée onto 6 dinner plates. Place the scallops on the purée, drizzle with the basil oil, and sprinkle with the chives. Serve warm.

sicilian grilled swordfish

SERVES 6

This was inspired by a Marcella Hazan recipe and I've made it into a one-dish meal. It's about as easy as dinner gets! The combination of meaty swordfish, peppery arugula, and lots of fresh lemon is wonderful.

2 tablespoons freshly squeezed lemon juice

¼ cup good olive oil

2 teaspoons minced fresh oregano leaves or 1 teaspoon dried oregano

Pinch of crushed red pepper flakes

Kosher salt and freshly ground black pepper

6 (½-inch-thick) swordfish steaks (5 to 6 ounces each)

4 ounces baby arugula

Grated zest of 1 lemon

Light a charcoal grill or preheat a gas or stovetop grill until very hot.

For the sauce, whisk together the lemon juice, olive oil, oregano, red pepper flakes, 1 tablespoon salt, and 1 teaspoon black pepper. Set aside.

When the grill is ready, sprinkle the fish with salt and pepper and cook over medium-high heat for 2 minutes on one side, then turn and cook for 1 to 2 minutes on the other side until almost cooked through. Remove to a flat dish, prick holes in the fish with the tines of a fork, and pour the lemon sauce over the fish while it's still hot. Sprinkle liberally with salt and pepper, cover with aluminum foil, and allow to rest for 5 minutes.

When ready to serve, place the swordfish on dinner plates or a serving platter, pile the arugula on top, drizzle with the sauce from the fish, and sprinkle with the grated lemon zest. Serve warm.

salmon & melting cherry tomatoes

SERVES 4

Le Bernardin in New York City is definitely one of the best restaurants in the country. The chef and co-owner Eric Ripert is a genius with fish; this was inspired by a dish he makes at the restaurant. The sweet salmon is delicious with the intensely flavored tomatoes, basil, and balsamic vinegar.

Good olive oil
1 cup chopped sweet onion, such as Vidalia
2 teaspoons minced garlic (2 cloves)
2 cups (1 pint) cherry or grape tomatoes, halved through the stem
  Kosher salt and freshly ground black pepper
1½ tablespoons good balsamic vinegar
1½ tablespoons julienned fresh basil leaves
1 (2-pound) salmon fillet, cut crosswise into 4 pieces

Preheat the oven to 425 degrees.

Heat 3 tablespoons of the olive oil in a medium (10-inch) sauté pan. Add the onion and sauté over medium-low heat for 5 minutes, stirring occasionally, until very tender but not browned. Add the garlic and sauté for 1 more minute. Stir in the tomatoes, 1 teaspoon salt, and ½ teaspoon pepper and cook over medium-low heat for 10 to 15 minutes, stirring occasionally, until the liquid evaporates and the tomato sauce thickens slightly. Off the heat, stir in the vinegar and basil.

Meanwhile, place a large (12-inch) cast-iron pan over high heat for 5 minutes. Brush the salmon all over with olive oil, sprinkle liberally with salt and pepper, and place it skin side up in the pan. Cook the fish for 3 to 4 minutes without moving them, until browned. Turn the salmon skin side down with a small metal spatula and transfer the pan to the oven for 8 minutes. (The salmon will not be completely cooked through.) Remove the fish to a serving platter, cover with aluminum foil, and allow to rest for 5 minutes.

Reheat the tomatoes, season to taste, and serve hot, warm, or at room temperature along with the salmon.

orecchiette with broccoli rabe & sausage

SERVES 6

This is a whole dinner in one pot—hearty pasta, spicy sausage, garlic, and lots of broccoli rabe. It's a terrific thing to make on the weekends because it reheats beautifully for a quick midweek meal. The shortcut here is to cook the pasta and the broccoli rabe together in the same pot.

½ pound sweet Italian pork sausages
½ pound hot Italian pork sausages
⅓ cup good olive oil
6 large garlic cloves, thinly sliced
2 (14.5-ounce) cans crushed tomatoes, preferably San Marzano
½ cup dry red wine
¼ cup tomato paste
  Kosher salt and freshly ground black pepper
1 pound dried orecchiette pasta
2 bunches broccoli rabe (2 to 2½ pounds total)
1 cup freshly grated Parmesan cheese, plus extra for serving

Preheat the oven to 350 degrees. Prick the sausages with a fork and place them on a sheet pan. Roast for 15 to 20 minutes, turning once, until just cooked through. Slice ½ inch thick and set aside.

Heat the olive oil over medium heat in a large, heavy pot or Dutch oven, such as Le Creuset. Add the sausage slices and sauté for 5 minutes, stirring frequently, until the pieces are browned. Add the garlic and cook for 1 minute. Add the tomatoes and their juices, the red wine, tomato paste, 2 teaspoons salt, and 1 teaspoon pepper and let the mixture simmer over low heat while you prepare the pasta and broccoli.

Bring a very large pot half filled with water to a boil and add 1 tablespoon of salt. Add the pasta and cook for 9 minutes exactly. While the pasta is cooking, trim the broccoli rabe to just below the leaves and discard the stems. Cut the leafy part of the broccoli rabe crosswise in

2-inch pieces. When the pasta has cooked for 9 minutes, add the broccoli rabe to the pasta and continue cooking for 2 to 3 minutes, until
the pasta is al dente and the broccoli is crisp-tender. Drain in a large
colander, reserving ⅓ cup of the cooking liquid, and add the pasta and
broccoli to the pot with the tomato and sausage mixture. Stir in the
Parmesan cheese and 1 teaspoon of salt. If the pasta seems dry, add
some of the reserved cooking liquid. Taste for seasonings, and serve
hot with extra Parmesan on the side.

lobster mac & cheese

SERVES 6 TO 8

A woman from Greenwich, Connecticut, cheerfully told me, "I made your Mac & Cheese for my fancy friends and they all went crazy!" Instead of that classic dinner from a box, it's the real thing made with aged Gruyère, sharp English Cheddar, and good pasta. For me, "foolproof" means making a dish I know well—with lots of variations, like adding lobster to my best Mac & Cheese.

2 tablespoons vegetable oil

Kosher salt

1 pound cavatappi or elbow macaroni

1 quart whole milk

8 tablespoons (1 stick) unsalted butter, divided

½ cup all-purpose flour

4 cups grated Gruyère cheese (12 ounces)

2 cups grated extra-sharp Cheddar (8 ounces)

½ teaspoon freshly ground black pepper

½ teaspoon ground nutmeg

1½ pounds cooked lobster meat, ½-inch-diced

1½ cups fresh white bread crumbs (5 slices, crusts removed)

Preheat the oven to 375 degrees.

Add the oil to a large pot of boiling salted water, add the pasta, and cook al dente according to the directions on the package. Drain well.

Heat the milk in a saucepan, but don't allow it to boil. In the large pot, melt 6 tablespoons of the butter and add the flour. Cook over low heat for 2 minutes, stirring constantly with a whisk. Still whisking, add the hot milk and cook for 1 to 2 minutes, until thickened and smooth. Off the heat, add the Gruyère, Cheddar, 1 tablespoon salt, the pepper, and nutmeg and stir until the cheese melts. Stir in the cooked pasta and lobster. Pile the mixture into 6 to 8 (2-cup) gratin dishes.

Melt the remaining 2 tablespoons of butter, combine with the bread crumbs, and sprinkle on top. Bake for 30 to 35 minutes, until the sauce is bubbly and the pasta is browned on top.

straw & hay
with gorgonzola

SERVES 3 TO 4

This dish is called paglia e fieno *or literally "straw and hay" because it usually calls for white and green pasta, which makes it look like fresh and dried hay. Of course, you can use any color pasta you like but I find it easiest to make with good tagliatelle. This is a rich, creamy dish flavored with prosciutto and my favorite Italian Gorgonzola.*

Cipriani dried pasta tastes just like fresh pasta.

There are two types of Gorgonzola: dolce is light and creamy and mountain is piquant and crumbly.

	Kosher salt
3	tablespoons unsalted butter, divided
4	ounces prosciutto, cut crosswise in ½-inch-thick matchsticks
1	cup chopped yellow onion (1 large)
1	tablespoon minced garlic (3 cloves)
1½	cups heavy cream
4	ounces Italian Gorgonzola dolce, crumbled
1½	teaspoons freshly ground black pepper
8 to 10	ounces tagliatelle or fettucine, such as Cipriani
2	cups frozen peas, defrosted (8 ounces)
½	cup freshly grated Parmesan cheese, plus extra for serving
¼	cup julienned fresh basil leaves

Fill a large pot with water, add 1 tablespoon of salt, and bring to a boil.

Meanwhile, melt 2 tablespoons of the butter in a large (12-inch) sauté pan over medium heat. Add the prosciutto and cook for 5 minutes, separating the slices with tongs, until crisp. Remove to a plate and set aside. Add the remaining tablespoon of butter and the onion to the sauté pan and cook for 5 minutes, stirring occasionally, until tender. Add the garlic and cook for 1 more minute. Add the cream, Gorgonzola, 1½ teaspoons salt, and the pepper and bring the sauce to a boil. Lower the heat and simmer for 5 minutes, until thickened. Turn off the heat.

When the sauce is almost done, add the pasta to the pot of boiling water and cook according to the package directions. Reserve 1 cup of the pasta water and drain the pasta, allowing some of the water to remain. Pour the pasta into the pan with the sauce. Add the peas, Parmesan, basil, and prosciutto and toss well. If the pasta seems dry, add some of the reserved pasta water. Taste for seasonings and serve hot with extra Parmesan.

penne alla vecchia bettola

SERVES 4

Nick & Toni's has been one of the great restaurants in East Hampton for about twenty years and this pasta has been on the menu the entire time! It's like the old standby penne alla vodka but with so much more flavor. Chef Joe Realmuto was kind enough to share the recipe with me, which originated from a restaurant in Florence that the owners loved. If you don't have a twelve-inch ovenproof sauté pan with a tight-fitting lid, you can use a Dutch oven or large pot.

I use San Marzano whole peeled canned tomatoes.

¼ cup good olive oil

2½ cups chopped Spanish onion (1 large)

1 tablespoon minced garlic (3 cloves)

½ teaspoon crushed red pepper flakes

1½ teaspoons dried oregano

1 cup vodka

2 (28-ounce) cans whole peeled plum tomatoes, drained (see note)
Kosher salt and freshly ground black pepper

¾ pound penne, such as De Cecco

2 tablespoons chopped fresh oregano leaves, plus extra for serving

1 cup heavy cream

½ cup freshly grated Parmesan cheese, plus extra for serving

Preheat the oven to 375 degrees.

Heat the oil in a large (12-inch) ovenproof sauté pan over medium heat. Add the onions and garlic and cook for about 5 minutes, until the onions are translucent. Add the red pepper flakes and dried oregano and cook for 1 more minute. Add the vodka and simmer for 5 to 7 minutes, until the mixture is reduced by half. Using clean hands, crush each tomato into the pan. Add 2 teaspoons of salt and ½ teaspoon of black pepper. Cover the pan with a tight-fitting lid, place in the oven, and bake for 1½ hours.

Bring a large pot of water to a boil. Add 2 tablespoons of salt and the pasta and cook according to the directions on the package. Drain and set aside.

Two cups at a time, carefully pour the tomato mixture into a blender and purée until smooth. Return the tomato mixture to the sauté pan (be careful; the handle is hot!). Add the fresh oregano, cream, 1 teaspoon salt, and ¼ teaspoon pepper and simmer partially covered for 10 minutes. Add the pasta to the sauce and cook for 2 more minutes. Stir in ½ cup of the Parmesan cheese and serve hot sprinkled with extra Parmesan and fresh oregano.

amelia's jambalaya

SERVES 8

*My friend Amelia Durand is from Louisiana and her family owns a general
store where they make all kinds of Southern specialties. Amelia is famous for her
jambalaya, which is the perfect one-dish dinner for a crowd. It has rice, shrimp,
spicy sausage, lots of vegetables—and I hope she doesn't mind that I've added
some chicken as well.*

2 tablespoons good olive oil

1½ pounds andouille or kielbasa sausage, sliced diagonally ½ inch thick

8 chicken thighs

Kosher salt and freshly ground black pepper

2 tablespoons unsalted butter

1½ cups yellow onion, chopped (1 large)

2 red bell peppers, seeded and large-diced

2 cups celery, large-diced (3 large stalks)

1 (28-ounce) can whole peeled plum tomatoes, drained and
medium-diced

2 tablespoons minced seeded jalapeño peppers (2 peppers)

1 tablespoon minced garlic (3 cloves)

2 tablespoons tomato paste

2 teaspoons dried oregano

1 teaspoon dried thyme

½ teaspoon ground cayenne pepper

1 cup dry white wine, such as Pinot Grigio

5 cups chicken stock, preferably homemade (page 62)

3 cups extra-long-grain white rice, such as Carolina

3 bay leaves

1 pound (16- to 20-count) shrimp, tails on, peeled and deveined

½ cup chopped fresh flat-leaf parsley, plus extra for garnish

½ cup sliced scallions, white and green parts, plus extra for garnish

¼ cup freshly squeezed lemon juice (2 lemons)

*To make in advance,
remove the lid to cool
before refrigerating
or the jambalaya
will keep cooking. To
reheat, add ½ cup
water and reheat with
the lid on over very low
heat on top of the stove.
Stir occasionally.*

Heat the olive oil in a very large (13-inch) Dutch oven or stockpot, add the sausage, and cook over medium heat for 8 to 10 minutes, turning the pieces until browned. Remove the sausage to a bowl with a slotted spoon. Meanwhile, pat the chicken dry with paper towels and sprinkle both sides liberally with salt and pepper. Add the chicken to the pot, skin side down, and cook over medium-high heat for 5 minutes, until browned. With tongs, turn and cook for another 5 minutes, until browned. Remove to the bowl with the sausage and set aside. Don't be tempted to cook both together; they won't brown properly.

Add the butter to the oil in the pot, then add the onions, bell peppers, celery, 1 tablespoon salt, and 1 teaspoon black pepper and cook over medium to medium-high heat for 10 minutes, until the onions are translucent. Add the tomatoes, jalapeño peppers, garlic, tomato paste, oregano, thyme, cayenne, and 1½ teaspoons salt, and cook for another 2 minutes. Add the white wine and scrape up the browned bits in the pot. Add the stock, rice, sausage, chicken, and bay leaves and bring to a boil. Cover the pot, reduce the heat to low, and simmer for 20 minutes. Stir in the shrimp and simmer covered for 5 more minutes. Off the heat, stir in the parsley, scallions, and lemon juice. Cover and allow to steam for 10 to 15 minutes, until the rice is tender and the shrimp are fully cooked. Discard the bay leaves, sprinkle with extra parsley and scallions, and serve hot.

vegetables

green beans gremolata

orange-braised carrots & parsnips

provençal cherry tomato gratin

crispy roasted kale

parmesan fennel gratin

sweet potato purée

spinach with feta & pine nuts

couscous with peas & mint

crispy english potatoes

truffled mashed potatoes

mushroom & leek bread pudding

brown rice & wheatberries

french flageolet beans

crusty basmati rice

balsamic-roasted brussels sprouts

foolproof thanksgiving

Thanksgiving is my favorite time of year. It feels like "the holidays" without all the pressure of Christmas. I love cooking Thanksgiving dinner, yet we ALL have a Thanksgiving disaster story—a friend's deep-fried turkey that was nicely browned on the outside but raw inside, the grilled turkey that landed on the gravel in the driveway, and the turkey that my friend roasted in an oven she had accidentally set on "clean." Oops! Frankly, for as much time as we spend *talking* about cooking turkeys, it's never the star of the meal—it's the side dishes that make Thanksgiving special. As someone once said, no one remembers the turkey—unless it's bad! Every year, I'm determined to make a meal that allows me to cook all my favorite dishes and to still have a good time at my own Thanksgiving dinner. These are my Thanksgiving guidelines:

1. Choose a menu that you can actually DO in the oven space that you have. Choose vegetables and side dishes like mashed potatoes or gratins that can be made in advance and kept warm on top of the stove or reheated in the oven in the half hour while the turkey rests.

2. Make a menu of recipes you feel totally comfortable cooking. This isn't the time to test that new herb and oyster stuffing that you've always wondered about.

3. The simplest turkey recipe is the best: make a dry salt and rosemary rub that soaks into the meat for a few days in the fridge. Then, the same way you roast a chicken, brush the skin with butter and sprinkle it generously with salt and pepper. Fill the cavity with a large onion quartered, a cut lemon, and a big bunch of fresh thyme. My foolproof recipe for Accidental Turkey is on page 120.

4. Use a meat thermometer! A 12- to 14-pound turkey will take 2 hours to cook. Roast until 165 degrees in the breast and 180 degrees in the thigh, take it out of the oven, and cover it tightly with aluminum foil to rest for 25 to 30 minutes. Carve it and serve drizzled with the pan juices. How easy is that?

5. Stuffing the turkey means it will take longer to cook, which in turn means the turkey will be drier. Instead, make a stuffing bread pudding, like my Mushroom & Leek Bread Pudding (page 188), and you'll have a succulent turkey *and* stuffing that's moist and crusty.

6. Don't serve appetizers before Thanksgiving dinner. Offer a glass of wine or Champagne plus some salted cashews and good olives. Your friends will thank you.

7. Ask each of your guests to bring a dessert. They'll feel that you trusted them to bring something special and then everyone gets to enjoy their favorite Thanksgiving dessert.

8. Make large quantities so you have leftovers. I send my guests home with extras so they can have turkey sandwiches the next day, which is half the pleasure of Thanksgiving.

9. Open and taste one bottle of the wine the day before Thanksgiving (it will only be better after it has had time to breathe). On Thanksgiving Day when all the liquor stores are closed isn't the time to realize that the wine is "corked" or bad.

10. Finally, if you ever have the urge to make Turducken (a boned chicken rolled inside a boned duck, inside a boned turkey), lie down until the urge passes!

green beans gremolata

SERVES 4 TO 6

Jeffrey loves French string beans so I'm always looking for new ways to prepare them. I blanch these and make the gremolata in advance and store them separately in the refrigerator. Then, just before dinner, I'll reheat the beans and toss on the topping with all the garlic, lemon zest, Parmesan, and pine nuts.

1 pound French green beans, trimmed
2 teaspoons minced garlic (2 cloves)
1 tablespoon grated lemon zest (2 lemons)
3 tablespoons minced fresh flat-leaf parsley
3 tablespoons freshly grated Parmesan cheese
2 tablespoons toasted pine nuts (see note)
2½ tablespoons good olive oil
Kosher salt and freshly ground black pepper

Toast pine nuts in a dry sauté pan over low heat for 5 to 10 minutes.

Bring a large pot of water to a boil. Add the green beans and blanch them for 2 to 3 minutes, until tender but still crisp. Drain the beans in a colander and immediately put them into a bowl of ice water to stop the cooking and preserve their bright green color.

For the gremolata, toss the garlic, lemon zest, parsley, Parmesan, and pine nuts in a small bowl and set aside.

When ready to serve, heat the olive oil in a large sauté pan over medium-high heat. Drain the beans and pat them dry. Add the beans to the pan and sauté, turning frequently, for 2 minutes, until coated with olive oil and heated through. Off the heat, add the gremolata and toss well. Sprinkle with ¾ teaspoon salt and ¼ teaspoon pepper and serve hot.

orange-braised carrots & parsnips

SERVES 6

This is a great winter vegetable dish to make in advance and reheat on top of the stove. Instead of roasting vegetables, braising infuses the carrots and parsnips with the flavors of shallots, orange, and fresh thyme and makes them incredibly tender.

1 pound carrots with the greens attached
1 pound thin parsnips
⅓ cup small-diced shallots (1 large)
2 teaspoons grated orange zest
1¼ cups freshly squeezed orange juice, divided (3 oranges)
⅓ cup good olive oil
6 sprigs fresh thyme, tied with kitchen string
Pinch of crushed red pepper flakes
Kosher salt and freshly ground black pepper
2 tablespoons minced fresh flat-leaf parsley, for serving

Preheat the oven to 275 degrees.

Trim and scrub or peel the carrots and parsnips. If the parsnips are thick, slice them in half or quarters lengthwise so they are about the same width as the carrots.

Place the carrots and parsnips in a pot or Dutch oven, such as Le Creuset, that's large enough for the vegetables to lie flat. Add the shallots, orange zest, ¾ cup of the orange juice, the olive oil, thyme, red pepper flakes, 2 teaspoons salt, and ½ teaspoon black pepper.

Place the pot on the stove and bring to a boil over medium-high heat. Cover tightly with a lid or heavy-duty foil. Transfer to the oven and cook for 1½ hours, until the carrots and parsnips are very tender. Discard the thyme bundle. Sprinkle with the remaining ½ cup of orange juice and the parsley and season to taste. Serve hot, warm, or at room temperature.

provençal cherry tomato gratin

I adore the flavors of Provence—tomatoes, garlic, thyme, and olive oil. Because you can always find decent cherry tomatoes and because roasting brings out their "summer" tomato flavor, this gratin is delicious all year long.

> 3 pints cherry or grape tomatoes, halved
> 1½ tablespoons plus ¼ cup good olive oil
> 1 teaspoon dried thyme
>   Kosher salt and freshly ground black pepper
> 3 large garlic cloves, peeled
> ⅓ cup chopped fresh flat-leaf parsley
> 2 cups coarse bread cubes from a country bread (crusts removed)

Preheat the oven to 400 degrees.

Place the tomatoes in a 9 × 13-inch ceramic dish. Add the 1½ tablespoons of olive oil, thyme, 1 teaspoon salt, and ½ teaspoon pepper and toss together. Spread the tomatoes evenly in the pan.

Place the garlic, parsley, and ½ teaspoon salt in the bowl of a food processor fitted with the steel blade and process until the garlic is finely chopped. Add the bread cubes and process until the bread is in crumbs. Add the ¼ cup of olive oil and pulse a few times to blend. Sprinkle the crumbs evenly over the tomatoes.

Bake the gratin for 40 to 45 minutes, until the crumbs are golden and the tomato juices are bubbling. Serve hot or warm.

crispy roasted kale

SERVES 6

This is the craziest vegetable dish! All you need to do is remove the little ribs from the curly kale (which you can do early in the day), toss the leaves with olive oil, salt, and pepper, and throw it in the oven. Fifteen minutes later you have a delicious crispy vegetable that's so good for you.

2 bunches curly kale (about 2½ pounds)
¼ cup good olive oil
Kosher salt and freshly ground black pepper
Fleur de sel

Preheat the oven to 350 degrees. Arrange 3 oven racks evenly spaced in the oven.

Lay each kale leaf on a board and, with a small sharp knife, cut out the hard stem. Tear large leaves in half. Place the kale in a large bowl of water and wash it well. Drain the kale and dry it in a salad spinner. Dry the bowl, and put the kale back in the bowl.

Toss the kale with the olive oil, 1 teaspoon kosher salt, and ½ teaspoon pepper. Divide the kale among 3 sheet pans or roast them in batches. If you put too much kale on one pan, it will steam rather than roast and will never become crisp. Roast for 15 minutes, until crisp. Sprinkle with fleur de sel and serve hot.

parmesan fennel gratin

SERVES 4 TO 6

Most fennel gratin recipes require boiling the fennel and then roasting it, but I found that stewing it in a covered gratin dish and then taking the lid off for the final baking was easier and had the same delicious results.

3 medium fennel bulbs

½ cup chicken stock, preferably homemade (page 62)

⅓ cup dry white wine

  Kosher salt and freshly ground black pepper

2 tablespoons unsalted butter, diced

3 tablespoons unsalted butter, melted

¾ cup panko (Japanese bread flakes)

1 cup freshly grated Parmesan cheese

1 tablespoon minced fresh flat-leaf parsley

1½ teaspoons grated lemon zest

To make in advance, prepare the dish completely and reheat it uncovered at 375 degrees for 15 minutes.

Preheat the oven to 375 degrees.

Remove the stalks from each fennel bulb and discard. Cut the bulbs in half lengthwise through the core. Remove most (but not all) of the core by cutting a V-shaped wedge, leaving the wedges intact. Cut each piece into 2, 3, or 4 wedges, depending on the size of the bulb. Arrange the wedges, cut side up, in a gratin dish just large enough to hold them snugly in a single layer. Pour the chicken stock and wine over the fennel, then sprinkle with 2 teaspoons of salt and ¾ teaspoon of pepper. Dot with the diced butter. Cover the dish tightly with aluminum foil and bake for 35 to 45 minutes, until the fennel is tender. Remove from the oven and raise the oven temperature to 425 degrees.

Meanwhile, make the topping. Combine the melted butter, panko, Parmesan, parsley, zest, 1 teaspoon salt, and ½ teaspoon pepper. Sprinkle evenly on top and return to the oven. Bake uncovered for 30 minutes, until the topping is browned. Serve hot or warm.

sweet potato purée

SERVES 6

There's a restaurant in Paris that makes the most sublime puréed potatoes. (I secretly think they use more cream than potatoes!) I decided to use a similar method to prepare these sweet potatoes. Some orange juice and cayenne pepper really enhance the distinct sweet potato flavor.

3 pounds sweet potatoes, peeled and cut into 1-inch chunks
½ cup half-and-half
1½ teaspoons grated orange zest
½ cup freshly squeezed orange juice
¼ teaspoon ground cayenne pepper
    Kosher salt and freshly ground black pepper
12 tablespoons (1½ sticks) unsalted butter, at room temperature

I use a rasp for zesting.

To make in advance, reheat in a bowl set over a pan of simmering water.

Place a steamer insert or a mesh colander in a large pot and add enough water to reach the bottom of the steamer. Place the sweet potatoes in the steamer and bring the water to a boil. Cover the pot, lower the heat, and cook over simmering water for about 25 minutes, until very tender. Check occasionally to be sure the water doesn't boil away.

Transfer the sweet potatoes to the bowl of an electric mixer fitted with the paddle attachment. With the mixer on low, slowly add the half-and-half, orange zest, orange juice, cayenne pepper, 1 tablespoon salt, and 1 teaspoon black pepper. With the mixer still on low, add the butter, 1 tablespoon at a time, until incorporated. Taste for seasonings and mix until smooth. Serve hot.

spinach with feta & pine nuts

SERVES 4

I love spinach and feta together. You sauté the spinach quickly in a large pan and then add lemon, feta, and pine nuts. I just put the sauté pan right on the buffet and let everyone help themselves.

> 2½ tablespoons good olive oil
> 1½ cups chopped yellow onion
> 1 lemon
> 1 pound fresh baby spinach leaves, washed, and spun dry
> Kosher salt and freshly ground black pepper
> 1½ tablespoons toasted pine nuts (page 169)
> ½ cup (½-inch) diced feta

Heat the olive oil in a large (12-inch) sauté pan, add the onion, and cook over medium heat for 8 to 10 minutes, until the onion is tender but not browned. Meanwhile, zest the lemon and set aside. Squeeze the lemon, add 1½ tablespoons of lemon juice to the pan. Add the spinach in big handfuls, tossing constantly with tongs for a minute or two until all the leaves are wilted. Toss with 1½ teaspoons salt and ½ teaspoon pepper and remove from the heat.

Add 1 teaspoon of the lemon zest, the pine nuts, and feta, and toss gently. Season to taste and serve hot.

couscous
with peas & mint

SERVES 8 TO 10

I love couscous. Not only is it delicious but when I'm having a dinner party, it's SO easy to make! I cook the shallots, add the chicken stock, and let it sit in the pot on the stove until 15 minutes before we sit down to eat. All I have to do is bring the stock to a boil, add the couscous, turn off the heat, and allow the couscous to steam for 10 minutes. At the last minute, add the peas, mint, and pine nuts, and dinner's ready.

2 tablespoons good olive oil

1 tablespoon unsalted butter

½ cup chopped shallots (2 large shallots)

3½ cups chicken stock, preferably homemade (page 62)

2 cups couscous

Kosher salt and freshly ground black pepper

12 ounces frozen peas, defrosted

½ cup julienned fresh mint leaves, loosely packed

⅓ cup toasted pine nuts (page 169)

Heat the oil and butter in a large saucepan over medium heat. Add the shallots and cook over medium-low heat for 4 minutes, stirring occasionally. Add the stock and bring to a boil. Stir in the couscous, 1 teaspoon salt, and ½ teaspoon pepper and put the lid on. Turn off the heat and allow the couscous to steam for 10 minutes. With a fork, fluff the couscous and stir in the peas, mint, and pine nuts. Season to taste. Depending on the saltiness of the chicken stock, you can add 1 more teaspoon of salt and ½ teaspoon of pepper. Serve hot.

crispy english potatoes

SERVES 6

This is a classic English way to prepare potatoes. You partially boil them, then drain them and shake them in the pan to rough up the edges. When you roast the roughed-up potatoes, the edges and skins get crusty along with the pancetta. Lots of salt makes it all taste even better.

2½ pounds Yukon Gold potatoes, unpeeled
  Kosher salt and freshly ground black pepper
3 ounces pancetta, ½-inch-diced
2 tablespoons good olive oil
¼ cup minced fresh flat-leaf parsley, for garnish

Preheat the oven to 425 degrees.

Cut the potatoes in 1- to 1½-inch chunks and place them in a large saucepan, preferably with 2 handles. Cover the potatoes with water by 1 inch and add 1 tablespoon of salt. Cover and bring the water to a boil. Uncover, lower the heat, and simmer for 10 minutes. Drain the water, leaving the potatoes in the pot. (The potatoes will have started cooking on the outside but will be hard inside.) Using a kitchen towel, grasp the pot with the lid on and shake the potatoes vigorously for a full 5 seconds to rough up the edges.

Meanwhile, 5 minutes before the potatoes are cooked, place the pancetta on a sheet pan and roast for 5 minutes. Add the drained potatoes, the olive oil, 1 teaspoon salt, and ½ teaspoon pepper to the pan and toss with a metal spatula. Roast the potatoes and pancetta for 45 minutes, tossing occasionally, until they are very browned and crisp. Don't worry if the skins come off—that's part of the crispiness. Sprinkle with parsley, salt, and pepper and serve hot.

truffled mashed potatoes

SERVES 6

These mashed potatoes are definitely foolproof. The potatoes are boiled, drained, and then mashed right in the pot with a hand mixer, which makes them so easy to prepare. I love the high-low combination of earthy potatoes and luxurious truffles. Truffle butter is one of my favorite ingredients; it's not terribly expensive and you can store it in the freezer.

2½ **pounds large Yukon Gold potatoes**

1½ **cups half-and-half**

6 **tablespoons (¾ stick) unsalted butter**

3 **ounces white truffle butter, at room temperature (see note)**

2 **tablespoons freshly grated Parmesan cheese**

Kosher salt and freshly ground black pepper

I buy truffle butter online at dartagnan .com and urbani.com.

Peel the potatoes and cut them in 1-inch chunks. Place them in a large, deep saucepan, cover with water, and bring to a boil. Lower the heat and simmer for 20 to 25 minutes, until very tender. Drain and return the potatoes to the saucepan.

Meanwhile, heat the half-and-half and butter in a small saucepan over medium heat until the butter melts. Off the heat, add the truffle butter and allow it to melt. If the butter doesn't melt completely, heat the mixture slightly but don't allow the truffles to cook!

With a hand mixer, beat the hot potatoes in the pot until they are broken up. Slowly beat in most of the hot truffle cream, the Parmesan, 2½ teaspoons salt, and 1 teaspoon pepper and beat until the potatoes are thick and smooth. (You may have some truffle cream left over; reserve it for reheating.)

To keep the potatoes hot or to reheat them, place them in a heat-proof bowl set over a pot of simmering water. Heat slowly, adding more truffle cream if the potatoes get too thick. Season to taste and serve hot.

mushroom & leek
bread pudding

A turkey with stuffing needs to cook longer than a plain turkey, so you end up with dry turkey and soggy stuffing. I prefer to roast a turkey the same way I roast a chicken, with just onion, lemon, and thyme in the cavity. Instead of stuffing, I make a savory bread pudding with mushrooms, leeks, and rich Gruyère cheese to go with the turkey. It's crusty on top and moist inside. Assemble this in advance and bake it before dinner.

Cut the leeks lengthwise, slice crosswise ¼ inch thick, wash in a big bowl of water, and spin-dry in a salad spinner.

Don't put mushrooms in water; wipe them with a clean, damp sponge.

6 cups (½-inch-diced) bread cubes from a rustic country loaf, crusts removed

2 tablespoons good olive oil

1 tablespoon unsalted butter

2 ounces pancetta, small-diced

4 cups sliced leeks, white and light green parts (4 leeks) (see note)

1½ pounds cremini mushrooms, stems trimmed and ¼-inch-sliced

1 tablespoon chopped fresh tarragon leaves

¼ cup medium or dry sherry

Kosher salt and freshly ground black pepper

⅓ cup minced fresh flat-leaf parsley

4 extra-large eggs

1½ cups heavy cream

1 cup chicken stock, preferably homemade (page 62)

1½ cups grated Gruyère cheese (6 ounces), divided

Preheat the oven to 350 degrees. Spread the bread cubes on a sheet pan and bake for 15 to 20 minutes, until lightly browned. Set aside.

Meanwhile, heat the oil and butter in a large (12-inch) sauté pan over medium heat. Add the pancetta and cook for 5 minutes, until starting to brown. Stir in the leeks and cook over medium heat for 8 to 10 minutes, until the leeks are tender. Stir in the mushrooms, tarragon, sherry, 1 tablespoon salt, and 1½ teaspoons pepper and cook for 10 to

12 minutes, until most of the liquid evaporates, stirring occasionally. Off the heat, stir in the parsley.

In a large mixing bowl, whisk together the eggs, cream, chicken stock, and 1 cup of the Gruyère. Add the bread cubes and mushroom mixture, stirring well to combine. Set aside at room temperature for 30 minutes to allow the bread to absorb the liquid. Stir well and pour into a 2½- to 3-quart gratin dish (13 × 9 × 2 inches). Sprinkle with the remaining ½ cup of Gruyère and bake for 45 to 50 minutes, until the top is browned and the custard is set. Serve hot.

brown rice
& wheatberries

SERVES 6

I love brown rice because it has so much more flavor than white rice. Here I've added some crunchy wheatberries to the nutty rice, plus scallions, onions, tart cranberries, and good chicken stock to give it lots of flavor. And how nice that it's also good for you!

> 2 tablespoons unsalted butter
> 2 tablespoons good olive oil
> 1½ cups chopped yellow onion (1 large)
> 1 cup brown rice, such as Texmati organic
> ½ cup hard red winter wheatberries (see note)
> 1 cup thinly sliced scallions, white and green parts (6 scallions),
>   plus extra for garnish
> ¼ cup toasted pine nuts (page 169)
> 3½ cups chicken stock, preferably homemade (page 62)
>   Kosher salt and freshly ground black pepper
> ½ cup dried cranberries

You can buy wheatberries at any health food store.

If you're short on oven space, you can simmer this dish on top of the stove instead.

Preheat the oven to 275 degrees.

Heat the butter and oil in a large pot or Dutch oven, such as Le Creuset. Add the onion and sauté over medium heat for 8 minutes, until translucent but not browned. Add the rice and wheatberries and continue to cook, stirring occasionally, for 5 minutes.

Stir in the scallions, pine nuts, chicken stock, 2 teaspoons salt, and 1 teaspoon pepper and bring to a boil. Stir, reduce the heat to a simmer, cover, and bake for 50 minutes. Stir in the cranberries, cover again, and set aside for 15 to 20 minutes, until the grains are tender and most of the liquid has been absorbed. Depending on the saltiness of the stock, add 1 teaspoon of salt and ½ teaspoon of black pepper to taste, sprinkle with sliced scallions, and serve hot.

french flageolet beans

SERVES 6 TO 8

These dried French beans are more delicately flavored than traditional Italian cannellini beans. Usually they simmer on top of the stove but if you throw them in a 300-degree oven you can set a timer and forget about it. If you're serving this with roasted meat, add the drippings from the roasting pan into the pot of cooked beans before you serve them to infuse the dish with the flavor of the roast.

1 pound dried flageolet beans
2 tablespoons good olive oil
4 ounces bacon, diced
2 cups medium-diced yellow onion (2 onions)
2 cups medium-diced fennel, trimmed and cored
2 carrots, scrubbed and medium-diced
4 teaspoons minced garlic (4 cloves)
2 cups canned beef or vegetable broth
2 bay leaves
1 large sprig fresh rosemary
Kosher salt and freshly ground black pepper

If you can't find flageolets in your local store, order them from ranchogordo.com.

The night before cooking, place the beans in a large bowl and cover them with water by 1 inch. Cover the bowl with plastic wrap and refrigerate overnight.

The next day, preheat the oven to 300 degrees. Drain the beans, rinse well, and drain again. In a large ovenproof pot such as Le Creuset, heat the olive oil over medium to medium-low heat, add the bacon, and cook for 4 to 5 minutes, until the bacon starts to brown. Add the onion, fennel, and carrots and cook for 7 minutes, stirring occasionally, until the vegetables begin to soften but aren't browned. Add the garlic and sauté for 1 to 2 more minutes.

Add the flageolets to the pot and stir in the broth, bay leaves, and rosemary. (Don't be tempted to add salt! The beans will become tough.) Add 2 cups of water, which should just cover the beans, and bring to a simmer on top of the stove. Cover the pot tightly and bake in the oven for 45 minutes. Remove the lid, stir in 1 tablespoon salt and 1 teaspoon pepper, and return the pot to the oven without the lid. Raise the temperature to 350 degrees and bake for 30 to 45 more minutes. The beans will be very tender and there will be just a little liquid in the bottom of the pan. (If the beans are dry, add a little more water.) Discard the bay leaves and rosemary. Taste for seasonings and serve hot.

crusty basmati rice

SERVES 4 TO 5

Axel Vervoordt is a great designer and antiques dealer in Antwerp, Belgium. He served a dish like this for lunch one day and I was dying to come home and recreate it. It's a combination of fluffy and crispy basmati rice, which is sometimes called Persian rice. I added fresh dill and pine nuts to give it lots of flavor.

- 1 tablespoon kosher salt
- 1½ cups basmati rice, such as Texmati organic
- 4 tablespoons (½ stick) unsalted butter
- ½ cup minced fresh dill, plus extra for serving
- ½ cup toasted pine nuts (page 169)
  Fleur de sel and freshly ground black pepper

In a large saucepan, bring 2 quarts of water to a boil and add the salt and rice. Bring the water to a boil, lower the heat, and simmer the rice for 10 minutes exactly, stirring occasionally to be sure it doesn't stick. Drain.

In a large heavy-bottomed pot, such as Le Creuset, melt the butter over medium-low heat. Spoon a third of the rice evenly over the butter without disturbing the butter, then sprinkle half the dill and half the pine nuts on the rice. In layers, add another third of the rice, then the remaining dill and pine nuts, and finally the rest of the rice on top. Cover the pot first with a clean kitchen towel and then with a heavy lid, folding the edges of the towel up over the lid so they won't catch on fire.

Cook the rice undisturbed over the lowest heat for 30 to 35 minutes, until the rice is tender and forms a golden crust on the bottom of the pot. Sprinkle with extra dill, 1 teaspoon fleur de sel, and ½ teaspoon pepper. Stir the crusty bits into the fluffy rice and serve hot.

balsamic-roasted brussels sprouts

SERVES 6

Tyler Florence has a terrific restaurant in San Francisco called Wayfare Tavern. It's warm and cozy and the food is very earthy. These crisp roasted Brussels sprouts with spicy pancetta and syrupy balsamic vinegar are inspired by a dish that I ate there. If the sprouts are very large, I cut them in quarters.

1½ pounds Brussels sprouts, trimmed and cut in half through the core
4 ounces pancetta, sliced ¼ inch thick
¼ cup good olive oil
   Kosher salt and freshly ground black pepper
1 tablespoon syrupy balsamic vinegar (see note)

Preheat the oven to 400 degrees.

Place the Brussels sprouts on a sheet pan, including some of the loose leaves, which get crispy when they're roasted. Cut the pancetta into ½-inch dice and add to the pan. Add the olive oil, 1½ teaspoons salt, and ½ teaspoon pepper and toss with your hands. Spread out the mixture in a single layer.

Roast the Brussels sprouts for 20 to 30 minutes, until they're tender and nicely browned and the pancetta is cooked. Toss once during roasting. Remove from the oven, drizzle immediately with the balsamic vinegar, and toss again. Taste for seasonings and serve hot.

You can buy aged balsamic vinegar that's syrupy—and very expensive—or you can boil good balsamic vinegar until reduced to half its volume and it will become syrupy as well.

desserts

chocolate cassis cake

perfect pound cake

raspberry crumble bars

carrot cake with ginger
mascarpone frosting

salted caramel brownies

pecan sandies

sticky toffee date cake
with bourbon glaze

pumpkin spice cupcakes
with maple frosting

german chocolate cupcakes

chocolate peanut butter globs

chocolate chunk blondies

stewed rhubarb & red berries

orange french lace cookies

prunes in armagnac

ultimate pumpkin pie with
rum whipped cream

perfect pie crust

maple pecan pie

rum raisin truffles

mexican hot chocolate

cinnamon baked doughnuts

viennese iced coffee

my oven

I have a love-hate relationship with my oven. I recently completed a renovation of my house. I had built it many years ago and it needed a face-lift (don't we all?). In addition to building a screened porch and opening up some walls, I decided to replace some kitchen appliances that had been working overtime for years. Choosing the stove was my toughest decision.

My old 48-inch stove had two average-size ovens that I used all the time. The newest models had replaced that arrangement with one huge oven and one small one. I could only think that the oven manufacturers decided that people needed to roast an enormous turkey once a year for Thanksgiving so they changed the configuration. Why??? The fact is the average cook will get more use from two regular-size ovens than one huge one and one tiny one, as I found out the hard way.

For one thing, I use half sheet pans for almost everything—baking, cooking, and roasting. The first time I gave a dinner party in the new kitchen, I realized that not only were my half sheet pans too big for the small oven, but in addition, a small oven doesn't have the same heat circulation a large one does so my dishes cooked very differently. Aarrggh. In essence I had one useable oven and one suitable only for rewarming dishes or heating plates.

That challenge made me realize what a luxury it had been to have two ovens for all those years. Of course, most kitchens have only one oven and people make wonderful dinner parties all the time. It made me think about menu planning in a new way.

The first thing I did was make sure that each meal had one dish that was prepared in advance, another that was baked or roasted in the oven, and a third cooked on top of the stove. For example, instead of serving three things that all roast in the oven—say, Slow-Roasted Filet of Beef with Basil Parmesan Mayonnaise, Provençal Cherry Tomato Gratin, and Crispy English Potatoes—I would roast the beef in the oven, sauté Spinach with Feta & Pine Nuts on top of the stove, and reheat Truffled Mashed Potatoes over a pan of simmering water on the stove. That way, the meat wasn't getting cold while I roasted the vegetables for dinner. If I still needed to cook two things in the oven at the same time, I did find that I could often cook the vegetables in advance (undercooking them a little) *before* the filet of beef and then, while the meat spent 15 minutes resting under aluminum foil, I reheated the Brussels sprouts in the same oven. No problem!

The second thing I realized about one oven is that if I'm roasting a chicken *and* carrots at the same time, it takes a little longer for them to cook than if they'd roasted alone. The heat simply doesn't circulate as well so I have to give things a little more time. I also found that if I have two dishes (cooking, not baking!), and one is supposed to cook at 400 degrees and the other at 350 degrees, they can both very happily do their thing together at 375 degrees, if I keep an eye on them.

Now I know that with a little extra menu planning, I can make all my favorite dishes in one oven—no problem!

chocolate cassis cake

SERVES 10 TO 12

*Chocolate, fresh berries, and crème de cassis liqueur are a delicious
combination—each ingredient makes the other one taste better. You can prepare
this rich chocolate cake early in the day, and then before dinner, simply toss the
berries in a little sugar and cassis to serve alongside.*

for the cake

    Baking spray with flour, such as Baker's Joy

12 tablespoons (1½ sticks) unsalted butter

10 ounces bittersweet chocolate, chopped (I use Perugina 60%)

½ cup unsweetened cocoa powder, such as Pernigotti

6 tablespoons crème de cassis liqueur

1 teaspoon pure vanilla extract

5 extra-large eggs, at room temperature

1 cup sugar

¼ teaspoon kosher salt

for the glaze

6 ounces bittersweet or semisweet chocolate, chopped

¼ cup heavy cream

2 to 3 tablespoons crème de cassis liqueur

½ teaspoon pure vanilla extract

to serve

2 (½ pint) boxes fresh raspberries

1 pint fresh strawberries, hulled and thickly sliced

⅓ cup sugar

⅓ cup crème de cassis liqueur

*Chocolate that is
labeled 60 to 70%
cacao is considered bit-
tersweet: the higher the
percentage of cacao,
the less sweet it will be.*

*Don't refrigerate this
cake or the glaze will
collect beads of water.*

For the cake, preheat the oven to 350 degrees. Spray a 9-inch round
springform pan with baking spray. Line the bottom of the pan with
parchment paper and spray it again with baking spray.

Melt the butter and chocolate together in a heat-proof bowl set over a pan of simmering water, stirring occasionally until smooth. Set aside to cool for 5 minutes. Whisk in the cocoa powder, cassis, and vanilla and set aside.

In the bowl of an electric mixer fitted with the whisk attachment (you can also use a hand mixer), beat the eggs, sugar, and salt on high speed for 3 to 5 minutes, until pale yellow and triple in volume. Pour the chocolate mixture into the egg mixture and carefully but thoroughly fold them together with a rubber spatula. Pour the batter into the prepared pan and bake for 35 to 40 minutes, until just barely set in the center. Allow to cool in the pan for 30 minutes and then release the sides of the pan. Invert the cake carefully onto a flat serving plate, remove the parchment paper, and cool completely.

For the glaze, melt the chocolate and cream together in a heat-proof bowl set over a pan of simmering water. Stir until smooth. Off the heat, whisk in the cassis and vanilla. Allow to cool for 10 minutes and spread over *just* the top of the cake.

Fifteen minutes before serving, toss the berries gently with the sugar and cassis. Cut the cake in wedges and serve with the berries on the side.

perfect pound cake

SERVES 12

I consider myself a pound cake aficionado. I love the simplicity of it: flour, sugar, butter, eggs, and vanilla. This recipe takes a bit of extra time to make because of the sifting but it really does make the texture more delicate. Serve it with tea in the afternoon or for dessert with some fresh berries and a dollop of crème fraîche.

Baking spray with flour, such as Baker's Joy
¼ cup demerara or turbinado sugar
3 cups sifted cake flour (see note)
1 teaspoon kosher salt
½ pound (2 sticks) unsalted butter, at room temperature (see note)
2½ cups granulated sugar
6 extra-large eggs, at room temperature
2 teaspoons pure vanilla extract
Seeds of 1 vanilla bean
2 teaspoons grated orange zest (2 oranges)
1 cup heavy cream

Measure sifted flour by spooning it lightly into the measuring cup.

If your kitchen is cooler than 72 degrees, you might have to soften the butter for a few seconds in a microwave.

DO NOT preheat the oven. Place a rack in the oven so the cake will sit in the center. Generously spray a 12-cup tube pan (not one with a removable bottom!) or two loaf pans (8 ½ × 4 ½ × 2 ½ inches) with the baking spray to coat evenly. Sprinkle with the demerara sugar, tilting the pan or pans to make an even coating of the sugar over the bottom and sides. Set aside.

Combine the sifted cake flour and salt and pass the mixture through a sieve or a sifter from one bowl into another THREE times. Set aside.

In the bowl of an electric mixer fitted with the paddle attachment, beat the butter and granulated sugar on medium speed for 5 minutes, until the mixture is light yellow and fluffy. With the mixer on medium-low, add the eggs one at a time, mixing well after each addition. Mix in the vanilla extract, vanilla seeds, and orange zest. With the mixer on low, add the flour mixture in thirds alternately with the cream, beginning and ending with flour and scraping down the sides of the bowl to combine. (Don't worry if it looks a little curdled.) Increase the speed to medium and beat for 3 minutes. The batter should be very light and fluffy.

Pour the batter into the prepared pans, smooth the top, and place in the cold oven. Turn the oven to 350 degrees and bake for 50 to 55 minutes, until a toothpick comes out clean. Cool in the pan for 30 minutes, carefully remove the cake to a baking rack, rounded side up, and allow to cool completely.

raspberry crumble bars

MAKES 9 TO 12 BARS

I love raspberries and shortbread together. The great thing about this recipe is that it uses one shortbread dough two ways: pat some in the bottom of the pan for the crust and the rest (with some granola added) becomes the crumble topping.

I use raspberry jam with seeds because I feel that it's more raspberry-like, but you can certainly use seedless jam as well.

½ pound (2 sticks) unsalted butter, at room temperature
¾ cup sugar
1 teaspoon pure vanilla extract
2⅓ cups all-purpose flour
½ teaspoon kosher salt
10 to 12 ounces good raspberry jam, such as Hero
⅔ cup good granola without dried fruit
¼ cup sliced almonds
Confectioners' sugar, for sprinkling

Preheat the oven to 350 degrees.

Place the butter and sugar in the bowl of an electric mixer fitted with the paddle attachment and mix on medium speed *just* until combined. With the mixer on low, add the vanilla.

Sift the flour and salt together and, with the mixer on low, slowly add to the butter mixture, mixing until it almost comes together in a ball. Turn the dough out on a board. Lightly pat two-thirds of the dough evenly on the bottom of a 9-inch square baking pan and about ¼ inch up the sides. Spread with the jam, leaving a ¼-inch border. Mix the granola into the remaining dough with your hands. Break the dough into small bits and distribute it on top of the jam, covering most of the surface. Sprinkle the almonds on top. Bake the bars for 45 minutes, until lightly browned.

Cool completely and cut into 9 or 12 bars. Sprinkle lightly with confectioners' sugar.

carrot cake with ginger mascarpone frosting

SERVES 8 TO 10

Rich carrot cake filled with raisins and nuts may be old-fashioned, but that's exactly what I like about it. I decided to update it by adding Italian mascarpone and some spicy crystallized ginger to the frosting. What a great combination that turned out to be!

      2 cups sugar

  1⅓ cups vegetable oil

      3 extra-large eggs, at room temperature

      1 teaspoon pure vanilla extract

      2 cups plus 1 tablespoon all-purpose flour

      2 teaspoons ground cinnamon

      2 teaspoons baking soda

  1½ teaspoons kosher salt

      1 pound carrots, grated (see note)

      1 cup raisins

      1 cup chopped walnuts
        Ginger Mascarpone Frosting (recipe follows)
        Crystallized ginger (not in syrup), chopped, for garnish

Grate the carrots by hand on a box grater; if you grate them in a food processor, the carrots will be too wet and the cake might fall.

Preheat the oven to 400 degrees. Grease 2 (9 × 2-inch) round cake pans, line the bottoms with parchment paper, and grease and flour the pans.

In the bowl of an electric mixer fitted with the paddle attachment, beat the sugar, oil, and eggs on medium-high speed for 2 minutes, until light yellow and thickened. Stir in the vanilla. In another bowl, sift together the 2 cups of flour, cinnamon, baking soda, and salt. With the mixer on low, slowly add the dry ingredients to the wet ones.

In a medium bowl, toss the carrots, raisins, walnuts, and the 1 table-spoon of flour. Stir into the batter with a rubber spatula. Divide the batter between the prepared pans and smooth the tops. Bake for 10 minutes, lower the heat to 350 degrees, and bake for 30 to 35 minutes, until a toothpick comes out clean. Cool in the pans for 15 minutes, turn out onto a baking rack, and cool completely.

Place one cake on a flat serving plate, rounded side down. Spread half the frosting on the top (not the sides). Place the second cake on top of the first cake, rounded side up. Frost just the top of the second cake. Sprinkle with the ginger and serve at room temperature.

ginger mascarpone frosting

FROSTS ONE 9-INCH CAKE

- 12 ounces Italian mascarpone cheese, at room temperature
- 4 ounces cream cheese, at room temperature
- 2 cups sifted confectioners' sugar
- 2 tablespoons heavy cream
- ½ teaspoon pure vanilla extract
- ⅓ cup minced crystallized ginger (not in syrup)
- ¼ teaspoon kosher salt

In the bowl of an electric mixer fitted with the paddle attachment, beat the mascarpone, cream cheese, confectioners' sugar, cream, and vanilla together for about 1 minute, until light and fluffy. Add the crystallized ginger and salt and beat for 30 seconds more.

salted caramel brownies

MAKES 12 LARGE BROWNIES

This is the perfect example of foolproof cooking. I took a recipe I could almost make in my sleep—Outrageous Brownies from The Barefoot Contessa Cookbook—*then added rich caramel sauce and flaked sea salt and came up with a whole new brownie. These are really dangerous; no one can stop eating them!*

½ pound (2 sticks) unsalted butter

8 ounces plus 6 ounces Hershey's semisweet chocolate chips

3 ounces unsweetened chocolate

3 extra-large eggs

1½ tablespoons instant coffee granules, such as Nescafé

1 tablespoon pure vanilla extract

1 cup plus 2 tablespoons sugar

½ cup plus 2 tablespoons all-purpose flour, divided

1½ teaspoons baking powder

½ teaspoon kosher salt

5 to 6 ounces good caramel sauce, such as Fran's

2 to 3 teaspoons flaked sea salt, such as Maldon

You'll want to find true caramel sauce rather than dulce de leche, which has a lot of milk or cream added. Fran's can be ordered at franschocolates.com.

It is very important to allow the batter to cool before adding the chocolate chips, or the chips will melt and ruin the brownies.

Preheat the oven to 350 degrees. Butter and flour a 9 × 12 × 1½-inch baking pan.

Melt the butter, 8 ounces of the chocolate chips, and the unsweetened chocolate together in a medium bowl set over simmering water. Allow to cool for 15 minutes. In a large bowl, stir (do not beat) together the eggs, coffee, vanilla, and sugar. Stir the chocolate mixture into the egg mixture and allow to cool to room temperature (see note).

In a medium bowl, sift together ½ cup of the flour, the baking powder, and salt and add to the chocolate mixture. Toss the remaining 6 ounces of chocolate chips and the remaining 2 tablespoons of flour in a medium bowl and add them to the chocolate mixture. Spread evenly in the prepared pan.

Bake for 35 minutes, until a toothpick comes out clean. Don't overbake!

As soon as the brownies are out of the oven, place the jar of caramel sauce without the lid in a microwave and heat just until it's pourable. Stir until smooth. Drizzle the caramel evenly over the hot brownies and sprinkle with the sea salt. Cool completely and cut into 12 bars.

pecan sandies

MAKES 22 TO 24 COOKIES

I love all kinds of shortbread. These classic holiday cookies get their wonderful flavor from demerara sugar, vanilla, and toasted pecans. You can make them early and store them in a sealed container.

1 cup pecan halves (4 ounces)

2 cups all-purpose flour, divided

¾ teaspoon kosher salt

½ teaspoon baking powder

½ pound (2 sticks) unsalted butter, at room temperature

½ cup demerara or turbinado sugar

2 teaspoons pure vanilla extract

24 whole pecan halves

The cooled cookies may be stored in an airtight container for several days.

Preheat the oven to 350 degrees.

Place the 1 cup of pecan halves on a sheet pan and bake for 5 to 10 minutes, until toasted. Set aside to cool.

Place the cooled pecans plus ¼ cup of the flour in a food processor fitted with the steel blade and process until the nuts are finely ground. Place the mixture in a medium bowl and add the remaining 1¾ cups of flour, the salt, and the baking powder. Stir to combine.

In the bowl of an electric mixer fitted with the paddle attachment, cream the butter and sugar on medium speed for 2 minutes, until light and fluffy. With the mixer on low, add the vanilla and the flour mixture, mixing just until the dough comes together.

Using a small ice cream scoop or your hands, form the batter into balls about 1 inch in diameter (1 ounce on a scale). Place the balls 1 inch apart on sheet pans lined with parchment paper. Press a pecan half into the center of each ball, pressing the pecan halfway down into the cookie. Bake for 20 to 25 minutes, until the cookies turn golden brown around the edges. Cool for 5 minutes. Place on a wire rack and cool completely.

sticky toffee date cake
with bourbon glaze

MAKES ONE 9-INCH CAKE

My friend Laura Donnelly has been the pastry chef at several wonderful restaurants in East Hampton and she also writes about food for The East Hampton Star. *When she's in the kitchen, Sticky Toffee Date Cake is always on the menu. It's a moist cake made with cooked dates and then soaked with a caramel sauce. I added good bourbon to her glaze.*

for the cake

¾ pound dates, pitted and chopped

1 teaspoon baking soda

¼ pound (1 stick) unsalted butter, at room temperature

⅓ cup granulated sugar

2 extra-large eggs, at room temperature

1 teaspoon pure vanilla extract

1¼ cups all-purpose flour

1 teaspoon kosher salt

1½ tablespoons baking powder

for the sauce

To make sweetened whipped cream, beat together 1 cup cold heavy cream, 1 table-spoon sugar, and ½ teaspoon pure vanilla extract in a mixer fitted with the whisk attachment until it makes soft peaks.

12 tablespoons (1½ sticks) unsalted butter

1 cup light brown sugar, lightly packed

½ cup heavy cream

¼ teaspoon kosher salt

2 tablespoons good bourbon, such as Maker's Mark

2 teaspoons pure vanilla extract

Sweetened whipped cream, for serving (see note)

Preheat the oven to 350 degrees. Butter and flour a 9 × 2-inch round cake pan.

Place the dates in a deep saucepan with 1¾ cups of water. Bring to boil, stirring a little to break up the dates. Allow to simmer for 1 minute. Off the heat, stir in the baking soda (it will bubble up!). Set aside.

Meanwhile, in an electric mixer fitted with the paddle attachment, cream the butter and granulated sugar on medium speed for 3 minutes, until light and fluffy. With the mixer on low, add the eggs, one at a time, and then the vanilla, scraping down the bowl. (The mixture may look curdled.) Combine the flour and salt and, with the mixer still on low, slowly add it to the batter. With the mixer on low, add the hot date mixture in two batches to the batter, scraping down the bowl. The batter will be runny but don't worry! Stir in the baking powder, which will also bubble up. Pour into the prepared pan. Bake for 30 to 35 minutes, until a toothpick inserted in the center comes out clean.

Meanwhile, combine the butter, brown sugar, heavy cream, and salt in a medium saucepan and bring to boil. Reduce the heat and simmer for 1 minute. Off the heat, stir in the bourbon and vanilla and pour into a 2-cup heat-proof glass measuring cup. Set aside.

As soon as the cake is done, poke holes all over it with a toothpick. Pour three-quarters of the sauce evenly over the cake while still warm and allow it to soak in for 30 minutes. Turn the cake out bottom side up onto a flat serving plate and pour the remaining sauce on top. Cool completely.

Serve at room temperature with sweetened whipped cream.

pumpkin spice cupcakes with maple frosting

MAKES 10 CUPCAKES

Pumpkin is a great base for cupcakes because it keeps the cake moist. I've added lots of pumpkin spices like cinnamon and ginger plus a frosting made with pure maple syrup. If you insist on making them even better, you can crumble some Heath bars on top for added crunch. These are great for a birthday party—grown-ups and kids both love them.

Canned pumpkin is actually better for baking than purée made from a fresh pumpkin. It's a different variety of pumpkin than our traditional jack-o'-lantern.

- ½ cup vegetable oil, plus extra for greasing the pan
- 1 cup all-purpose flour
- 1 teaspoon baking powder
- ½ teaspoon baking soda
- 1 teaspoon ground cinnamon
- ½ teaspoon ground ginger
- ½ teaspoon ground nutmeg
- ½ teaspoon kosher salt
- 2 extra-large eggs, at room temperature
- 1 cup canned pumpkin purée (not pie filling)
- ½ cup granulated sugar
- ½ cup light brown sugar, lightly packed
- Maple Frosting (recipe follows)
- ½ cup coarsely chopped Heath bars, for serving (two 1.4-ounce bars)

Preheat the oven to 350 degrees. Brush the top of a muffin pan with vegetable oil and line it with 10 paper liners.

Into a medium bowl, sift together the flour, baking powder, baking soda, cinnamon, ginger, nutmeg, and salt. In a larger bowl, whisk together the eggs, pumpkin, granulated sugar, brown sugar, and the ½ cup vegetable oil. Add the flour mixture and stir to combine.

Scoop the batter into the prepared tins (I use a 2¼-inch ice cream scoop) and bake for 20 to 25 minutes, until a toothpick comes out clean. Cool completely, spread the cupcakes with the Maple Frosting, and sprinkle with the chopped Heath bars.

maple frosting

FROSTS 10 CUPCAKES

6 ounces cream cheese, at room temperature

3 tablespoons unsalted butter, at room temperature

2 tablespoons pure maple syrup

½ teaspoon pure vanilla extract

2 cups sifted confectioners' sugar

Be sure the cream cheese and butter are absolutely at room temperature or the frosting will be lumpy. I leave them on the counter overnight.

In the bowl of an electric mixer fitted with the paddle attachment, cream the cream cheese, butter, maple syrup, and vanilla on medium-low speed until very smooth. With the mixer on low, slowly add the confectioners' sugar and mix until smooth.

german chocolate cupcakes

MAKES 14 TO 15 CUPCAKES

The name of these cupcakes is not because they're German but because they were meant to be made with German brand unsweetened chocolate. Instead, I use dark Italian cocoa powder. The cake is rich and chocolaty and the frosting is loaded with coconut, almonds, and pecans. It's a classic . . . updated.

12 tablespoons (1½ sticks) unsalted butter, at room temperature
⅔ cup granulated sugar
⅔ cup light brown sugar, lightly packed
2 extra-large eggs, at room temperature
2 teaspoons pure vanilla extract
1 cup buttermilk, shaken, at room temperature
½ cup sour cream, at room temperature
2 tablespoons freshly brewed coffee
1¾ cups all-purpose flour
1 cup unsweetened cocoa powder, such as Pernigotti
1½ teaspoons baking soda
½ teaspoon kosher salt
Coconut Frosting (recipe follows)

Preheat the oven to 350 degrees. Line cupcake pans with 14 or 15 paper liners.

In the bowl of an electric mixer fitted with the paddle attachment, cream the butter, granulated sugar, and brown sugar on medium-high speed for 5 minutes, until light and fluffy. Scrape down the bowl. Lower the speed to medium, add the eggs one at a time, then add the vanilla and mix well. In a separate bowl, whisk together the butter-milk, sour cream, and coffee. In a third bowl, sift together the flour, cocoa powder, baking soda, and salt. With the mixer on low, add the buttermilk and flour mixtures alternately in thirds, beginning with the buttermilk and ending with the flour. Don't overmix! Fold the batter a few times with a rubber spatula to be sure it's mixed.

Scoop the batter into the cupcake liners. (I use a 2¼-inch ice cream scoop.) Bake in the center of the oven for 20 to 25 minutes, until a toothpick comes out clean. Cool for 10 minutes, remove from the pans, and allow to cool completely before frosting.

coconut frosting

FROSTS 14 TO 15 CUPCAKES

- 12 tablespoons (1½ sticks) unsalted butter
- 1 (12-ounce) can evaporated milk
- 1¼ cups light brown sugar, lightly packed
- 4 extra-large egg yolks
- 1 teaspoon pure vanilla extract
- ½ teaspoon pure almond extract
- 2 cups sweetened flaked coconut
- 1 cup blanched sliced almonds, toasted (see note)
- 1 cup chopped pecans
- ¼ teaspoon kosher salt

To toast the almonds, bake them in a single layer on a sheet pan in a 375-degree oven for 5 to 10 minutes, tossing once to brown evenly.

Melt the butter in a large saucepan over medium heat. Whisk in the evaporated milk, brown sugar, and egg yolks and bring to a simmer over medium heat. Simmer, stirring constantly with a wooden spoon, for about 15 minutes, until slightly thickened. If the mixture looks a bit curdled, beat it vigorously with a whisk. Off the heat, stir in the vanilla extract, almond extract, coconut, almonds, pecans, and salt. Allow to cool for about an hour. Frost the cupcakes with a knife or small metal spatula.

chocolate peanut butter globs

MAKES 20 TO 22 COOKIES

There was an amazing restaurant in New York City in the 1980s called Soho Charcuterie. They used to make these huge, moist, dense double-chocolate cookies called Chocolate Globs, which were actually the inspiration for my Outrageous Brownies. I've added peanut butter chips to the original recipe and I think it's even more outrageous!

To make in advance, wrap the cookies well and store for up to 24 hours at room temperature.

6	tablespoons (¾ stick) unsalted butter
12	ounces semisweet chocolate chips, divided
2	ounces unsweetened chocolate
2	extra-large eggs
1	tablespoon instant espresso powder, such as Medaglia d'Oro
2	teaspoons pure vanilla extract
¾	cup sugar
⅓	cup plus 1 tablespoon all-purpose flour
1	teaspoon baking powder
¼	teaspoon kosher salt
1	cup whole walnut halves (*not* chopped)
1	cup whole pecan halves (*not* chopped)
⅔	cup peanut butter chips, such as Reese's

Preheat the oven to 325 degrees. Line a few sheet pans with parchment paper.

In a bowl set over simmering water, melt the butter, 6 ounces of the chocolate chips, and the unsweetened chocolate, stirring occasionally, until just melted. Remove from the heat and cool for 15 minutes.

In the bowl of an electric mixer fitted with the paddle attachment, beat the eggs, espresso powder, and vanilla until combined. Add the sugar, raise the speed to medium-high, and beat for 2 minutes, until the batter is thick and falls back on itself in a ribbon. Set aside.

With the mixer on low, slowly add the chocolate mixture to the egg mixture. Combine the ¹/₃ cup of flour, baking powder, and salt in a small bowl and fold it into the chocolate mixture with a rubber spatula. In another bowl, combine the walnuts, pecans, peanut butter chips, the remaining 6 ounces of chocolate chips, and the tablespoon of flour and fold it into the chocolate mixture. With 2 soup spoons, drop rounded mounds of batter 1 inch apart onto the prepared sheet pans. Bake for 15 minutes exactly. Cool on the baking sheets.

chocolate chunk blondies

MAKES 12 LARGE BARS

Who doesn't love chocolate chunk cookies? This is the same thing — made into bars. Blondies have a tendency to be dry but there are two solutions: underbake them a little and store them in the fridge wrapped tightly with plastic wrap. Chocolate chunks have a more intense chocolate flavor than chips. Moist delicious blondies, every time!

 ½ pound (2 sticks) unsalted butter, at room temperature
  1 cup light brown sugar, lightly packed
 ½ cup granulated sugar
  2 teaspoons pure vanilla extract
  2 extra-large eggs, at room temperature
  2 cups all-purpose flour
  1 teaspoon baking soda
  1 teaspoon kosher salt
 1½ cups chopped walnuts
 1¼ pounds semisweet chocolate chunks, such as Nestlé's

Preheat the oven to 350 degrees. Grease and flour an 8½ × 12 × 2-inch baking pan.

In the bowl of an electric mixer fitted with the paddle attachment, cream the butter, brown sugar, and granulated sugar on high speed for 3 minutes, until light and fluffy. With the mixer on low, add the vanilla. Add the eggs, one at a time, and mix well, scraping down the bowl after each addition. In a small bowl, sift together the flour, baking soda, and salt. With the mixer still on low, slowly add the flour mixture to the butter mixture. Fold in the walnuts and chocolate chunks with a rubber spatula.

Spread the batter into the prepared pan and smooth the top. Bake for 30 minutes, until a toothpick comes out clean. Don't overbake! The toothpick may have melted chocolate on it but it shouldn't have wet batter. Cool completely in the pan and cut into 12 bars.

stewed rhubarb
& red berries

SERVES 6

Rhubarb is only in season for a short time in the spring but it's worth waiting for. I love to stew it with lots of sweet red berries and a hint of Grand Marnier. It's also good for breakfast over Greek yogurt. You can make this compote several days in advance and store it in the refrigerator.

2 pounds fresh rhubarb cut in ¾-inch chunks (6 to 8 cups)

1 cup sugar

½ teaspoon kosher salt

1 pint fresh or frozen strawberries, hulled and thickly sliced

½ pint fresh or frozen raspberries

⅓ cup freshly squeezed lemon juice (2 lemons)

⅓ cup freshly squeezed orange juice (2 oranges)

2 tablespoons Grand Marnier or Triple Sec liqueur (optional)

Sweetened whipped cream or vanilla ice cream, for serving

Place the rhubarb in a large saucepan and add the sugar, salt, and ⅔ cup water. Bring to a boil over high heat, then lower the heat and simmer for about 10 minutes, stirring occasionally, until the rhubarb is tender and starts to fall apart. Remove from the heat, stir in the strawberries, raspberries, lemon juice, orange juice, and Grand Marnier, if using, and allow to cool. Serve warm, at room temperature, or cold with a dollop of whipped cream or a scoop of ice cream.

orange french lace cookies

MAKES 30 TO 36 COOKIES

My friend Sarah Chase writes wonderful cookbooks. These cookies are inspired by a recipe from her Nantucket Open-House Cookbook. *They're thin and crisp with lots of toasted almonds and a hint of orange. They can be stored for days in a sealed container.*

2 cups blanched sliced almonds (see note)
1 cup all-purpose flour
¼ pound (1 stick) unsalted butter
⅔ cup light brown sugar, lightly packed
⅓ cup light corn syrup
2 tablespoons frozen orange juice concentrate, defrosted
2 teaspoons grated orange zest
1 teaspoon pure vanilla extract

Blanched sliced almonds are the ones that are thinly sliced and have the skins removed.

Preheat the oven to 375 degrees. Line 2 sheet pans with parchment paper.

Place the almonds on a sheet pan and toast them for 5 to 10 minutes, until lightly browned, tossing once to toast evenly. Place 1 cup of the toasted almonds in a food processor fitted with the steel blade and chop them very coarsely. (Reserve the rest for later.) Combine the chopped almonds with the flour and set aside.

Meanwhile, place the butter, brown sugar, corn syrup, orange juice concentrate, orange zest, and vanilla in a small saucepan and bring to a boil over medium heat. Off the heat, gradually whisk in the flour mixture until thoroughly combined. Stir in the reserved toasted almonds.

With 2 teaspoons (tableware rather than measuring spoons), drop rounded spoonfuls of batter (about 1½ inches wide) onto the prepared sheet pans, spacing them at least 2 inches apart. (I put 8 on each pan.)

Bake for 7 to 9 minutes, until the edges are golden brown, turning the pans in the oven to brown evenly. Allow to cool and transfer to a wire rack. Repeat for the remaining batter. Store the cooled cookies in an airtight container between layers of wax or parchment paper.

prunes in armagnac

SERVES 6 TO 8

My friend Barbara Liberman and I travel a lot together and whenever we see prunes in Armagnac on the menu, we have to order it. At restaurants in Paris they bring you a big bowl and you help yourself with a drizzle of cream or dollop of crème fraîche. At home, I serve the prunes warm with a scoop of ice cream melting into them. Good tea and a whole vanilla bean are the two secret ingredients.

3 spiced tea bags, such as Mariage Frères or Constant Comment
4 cups extra-large pitted prunes (18 to 20 ounces), such as Sunsweet Premium
⅓ cup honey, plus extra for serving
1½ cups Armagnac, plus extra for serving
1½ teaspoons pure vanilla extract
1 cup freshly squeezed orange juice (3 oranges)
1 vanilla bean, split in half lengthwise
2 (3-inch) cinnamon sticks
2 lemons
2 pints honey vanilla ice cream, softened for serving

Armagnac is very good brandy from the Gascony region of France.

Place 3 cups of water in a medium saucepan and bring to a boil. Turn off the heat, add the tea bags, and steep for 5 minutes. Discard the tea bags, add the prunes and honey, turn the heat to medium-high, and bring to a boil. Lower the heat and simmer uncovered for 3 minutes to plump the prunes.

Pour the prunes and all the liquid into a medium bowl and stir in the Armagnac, vanilla, orange juice, vanilla bean, and cinnamon sticks. With a vegetable peeler, cut 4 large strips of zest from 1 lemon and add to the mixture. Cut the lemon in half, cut 4 (¼-inch-thick) slices, and add to the bowl. Cover the bowl with plastic wrap and set aside at room temperature for 6 to 12 hours. (If you're not serving the prunes that day, refrigerate them in their liquid.)

To serve, place the prunes in shallow dessert bowls and serve cold, at room temperature, or slightly warmed, spooning the macerating liquid over them. Add a scoop of ice cream, a drizzle of Armagnac, a drizzle of honey, and a sprinkling of grated lemon zest. (You'll be surprised how much flavor this adds!) Serve immediately.

ultimate pumpkin pie
with rum whipped cream

SERVES 8 TO 10

Pumpkin pie can be boring and dense so I set out to make a better pumpkin pie. Pumpkin has a distinct squash flavor that you want to enhance without overpowering it. I've filled the prebaked crust with a lightly spiced pumpkin mixture that tastes more like a mousse than a dense custard. Dark rum and grated orange zest are my secret ingredients.

1 unbaked Perfect Pie Crust (page 244)
Dried beans, for blind baking

filling

1 (15-ounce) can pumpkin purée (not pie filling)
½ cup light brown sugar, lightly packed
¼ cup granulated sugar
½ teaspoon ground cinnamon
¼ teaspoon ground ginger
¼ teaspoon ground nutmeg
½ teaspoon kosher salt
2 teaspoons grated orange zest
3 extra-large eggs, lightly beaten
1 cup heavy cream
½ cup whole milk
2 tablespoons dark rum, such as Mount Gay
Rum Whipped Cream (recipe follows)

Preheat the oven to 425 degrees.

Line an 11-inch pie pan with the unbaked pie crust and place it on a sheet pan. Line the crust with parchment paper. Fill the paper three-quarters full with the beans and bake the crust for 15 minutes, until the edges start to brown. Remove the beans and paper (save the beans for another time), prick the crust all over with the tines of a fork, and bake for another 5 minutes.

Reduce the oven temperature to 350 degrees.

Meanwhile, in a large bowl, whisk together the pumpkin, brown sugar, granulated sugar, cinnamon, ginger, nutmeg, salt, orange zest, eggs, cream, milk, and rum. Pour the filling into the baked pie shell. Bake for 55 to 65 minutes, until the filling is just set in the middle and a knife inserted in the center comes out clean. Set aside to cool completely. Serve with the rum whipped cream.

rum whipped cream

SERVES 8 TO 10

A dollop of mascarpone or crème fraîche in whipped cream stabilizes it so you can make it in advance and store it in the fridge without it separating.

If you overwhip the cream and it looks curdled, just add a little more cream and whip it until it forms soft peaks.

- 1 **cup cold heavy cream**
- 3 **tablespoons sugar**
- 1 **tablespoon mascarpone or crème fraîche**
- 1 **tablespoon good dark rum, such as Mount Gay**
- 1 **teaspoon pure vanilla extract**

Place the cream in the bowl of an electric mixer fitted with the whisk attachment and beat on medium speed for 1 minute. Add the sugar, mascarpone, rum, and vanilla and beat on medium-high until it forms soft peaks. Serve with the pumpkin pie.

perfect pie crust

MAKES TWO (9- TO 11-INCH) CRUSTS

There are a few tricks to making perfect pie crust. First, the butter, shortening, and water need to be ice cold. When you roll out the dough, you want to see bits of butter throughout. Second, allow the dough to relax in the fridge for at least thirty minutes before rolling it out. And third, don't stretch the dough at all when you ease it into the pan. Perfect pie crust every time!

12 tablespoons (1½ sticks) very cold unsalted butter

3 cups all-purpose flour

1 tablespoon sugar

1 teaspoon kosher salt

⅓ cup very cold vegetable shortening, such as Crisco

½ cup ice water

I store the shortening in the refrigerator so it's always cold.

You can store the prepared pie crust in the fridge for up to a day.

Cut the butter in ½-inch dice and return it to the refrigerator while you prepare the flour mixture. Place the flour, sugar, and salt in the bowl of a food processor fitted with a steel blade and pulse a few times to mix. Add the butter and shortening. Pulse 8 to 12 times, until the butter is the size of peas. With the machine running, pour the ice water down the feed tube and pulse the machine until the dough begins to form a ball. Dump out onto a floured board and roll into a ball. Wrap in plastic wrap and refrigerate for 30 minutes.

Cut the dough in half. Roll each piece on a well-floured board into a circle at least 1 inch larger than the pie pan, rolling from the center to the edge, turning and flouring the dough so it doesn't stick to the board. (You should see bits of butter in the dough.) Fold the dough in half, ease it into the pie pan without stretching at all, and unfold to fit the pan. With a small sharp paring knife, cut the dough 1 inch larger around than the pan. Fold the edge under and crimp the edge with either your fingers or the tines of a fork.

maple pecan pie

SERVES 8

This recipe is inspired by a recipe I found in the wonderful magazine Real Simple. *I usually find pecan pie too sweet but this one has real depth of flavor from honey, maple syrup, bourbon, and orange zest. This is definitely our new family tradition for Thanksgiving! (Not to mention it takes no time to make.)*

- 1 unbaked Perfect Pie Crust (page 244)
- ½ cup light corn syrup
- ¼ cup good honey
- ¼ cup pure maple syrup
- 4 tablespoons (½ stick) unsalted butter, melted
- 3 extra-large eggs, lightly beaten
- 1 tablespoon bourbon, such as Maker's Mark
- ½ teaspoon pure vanilla extract
- ½ teaspoon grated orange zest
- ½ teaspoon kosher salt
- 2½ cups whole pecan halves (9 ounces)

Preheat the oven to 350 degrees.

Line a 9-inch pie pan with the pie crust. Place it on a sheet pan.

In a large bowl, whisk together the corn syrup, honey, maple syrup, butter, eggs, bourbon, vanilla, orange zest, and salt. Stir in the pecans and pour into the unbaked pie shell. Bake for 50 to 55 minutes, until the center is just set. Set aside to cool, and serve.

rum raisin truffles

MAKES 35 TO 40 TRUFFLES

My friend Brigitte Browney owns a company called Cocoa Pod Chocolates and she makes the most amazing creations like white chocolate pumpkins filled with lots of her delicious truffles. She made these rum raisin truffles with me and I love them. They're richly flavored with sweet rum and raisins. No one will believe you made your own truffles.

½ cup heavy cream

1 tablespoon unsalted butter

26 ounces good milk chocolate, chopped, divided

1½ ounces raisins (about 2 tablespoons)

¼ cup dark rum, such as Mount Gay

I use Callebaut milk chocolate.

Chocolate truffles will last tightly wrapped at room temperature for about a week.

In a heat-proof bowl set over simmering water, heat the cream until hot to the touch but not boiling and turn off the heat. Add the butter and 12 ounces of the chocolate to the hot cream. Stir until the chocolate melts. Meanwhile, mince the raisins and combine them with the rum in a small bowl. Stir the raisins and rum mixture into the melted chocolate mixture, cover with plastic wrap, and set aside at room temperature for 6 hours or overnight.

The next day, using a very small (1¼-inch) ice cream scoop (you can also use 2 spoons), scoop balls of the mixture onto sheet pans lined with parchment paper. Refrigerate for at least 30 minutes.

When the chocolate is cold, place 10 ounces of the remaining chocolate in a small glass bowl and heat it in a microwave on high for 20 seconds exactly. Stir the chocolate and continue to heat in the microwave for 20 seconds at a time, stirring in between, until the chocolate is smooth and shiny. This will take 5 or 6 times, depending on your microwave. Add the remaining 4 ounces of chocolate and stir until smooth. The chocolate should be 85 to 90 degrees on an instant-read thermometer. If it's too cool, heat it briefly in the microwave. You'll want it to be pourable.

Using 2 spoons, pick up a chilled ball in one spoon and warm chocolate in the other and roll them around together until the chilled ball is completely coated in warm chocolate (don't drop the ball into the chocolate or the warm chocolate will cool off!). Place the coated truffle back on the parchment paper. Continue coating the balls until they're all covered with milk chocolate. Allow to sit at room temperature until the chocolate hardens. Serve at room temperature.

mexican hot chocolate

MAKES 2 TO 3 CUPS

I love to shake things up, so in winter, when everyone expects my usual apple crisp for dessert, I surprise them and serve big mugs of spicy hot chocolate with a cinnamon doughnut for dipping. The hot chocolate is made with brown sugar, vanilla, cinnamon, and a surprising hint of cayenne pepper.

     2 cups whole milk
     1 tablespoon light brown sugar
  4½ ounces bittersweet chocolate, chopped
     ½ teaspoon pure vanilla extract
   ¹/₈ teaspoon ground cinnamon
     Small pinch of ground cayenne pepper
     Long cinnamon sticks for stirrers (optional)

for serving

     Cinnamon Baked Doughnuts (recipe follows)
     or store-bought cinnamon doughnuts

I like Lindt bittersweet chocolate.

Place the milk and brown sugar in a medium saucepan and bring just to a simmer. Off the heat, whisk in the chocolate, vanilla, cinnamon, and cayenne pepper. Allow to steep for 3 minutes. Reheat the mixture over low heat until it almost comes to a simmer.

Pour into mugs, add cinnamon stirrers, if using, and serve with cinnamon doughnuts for dipping.

cinnamon baked doughnuts

MAKES 12 DOUGHNUTS

While there's nothing like a fresh doughnut hot out of the fryer, they can also be a little greasy. I researched baked doughnuts and came up with this one that is every bit as satisfying as a fried doughnut and oh, so delicious! They're great with hot chocolate for dessert or with coffee for Sunday breakfast.

Baking spray with flour, such as Baker's Joy

2 cups all-purpose flour

1½ cups sugar

2 teaspoons baking powder

1 teaspoon ground cinnamon

½ teaspoon ground nutmeg

½ teaspoon kosher salt

1 extra-large egg, lightly beaten

1¼ cups whole milk

2 tablespoons unsalted butter, melted

2 teaspoons pure vanilla extract

for the topping

8 tablespoons (1 stick) unsalted butter

½ cup sugar

½ teaspoon ground cinnamon

Preheat the oven to 350 degrees. Spray 2 doughnut pans well.

Into a large bowl, sift together the flour, sugar, baking powder, cinnamon, nutmeg, and salt. In a small bowl, whisk together the egg, milk, melted butter, and vanilla. Stir the wet mixture into the dry ingredients until just combined.

Spoon the batter into the baking pans, filling each one a little more than three-quarters full. Bake for 17 minutes, until a toothpick comes out clean. Allow to cool for 5 minutes, then tap the doughnuts out onto a sheet pan.

For the topping, melt the 8 tablespoons of butter in an 8-inch sauté pan. Combine the sugar and cinnamon in a small bowl. Dip each doughnut first in the butter and then in the cinnamon sugar, either on one side or both sides.

viennese iced coffee

SERVES 4

My friend Frank Newbold went to Vienna and described a frozen coffee drink that he was served with a scoop of ice cream. That's not what I want to drink for breakfast but I thought if I added a little sugar, vanilla, and a dusting of cocoa powder, it would make a really delicious—and fast!—dessert. Coffee and dessert all in one!

6 (1-ounce) shots of espresso, regular or decaf

3 tablespoons sugar

1 teaspoon pure vanilla extract

¼ cup hot water

2 cups ice

4 scoops vanilla or coffee ice cream

Unsweetened cocoa powder, such as Pernigotti

Short straws, for serving

Combine the espresso, sugar, vanilla, and hot water in a blender and stir until the sugar dissolves. Put the ice in the blender and process on high until the mixture is almost completely smooth. Divide the mixture between 4 short glasses.

Place the ice cream in a microwave on high for 15 seconds, until softened. Scoop one ball of ice cream into each glass. With a small sifter, sprinkle each drink lightly with cocoa powder. Serve with a short straw and a teaspoon.

12 foolproof tips
for table settings

Use non-skid rug mats as table
protectors—you cut them with
a pair of scissors!

Arrange one flower in abundance
down the table.

Use mismatched glasses in
the same shape.

Make deconstructed bouquets—lots
of small vases with one type
of flower in each vase.

Mix modern and flea market
linens and china.

Use kitchen towels for
casual napkins.

With square plates, line
everything up squarely.

For fancier settings, use elegant
French kitchen towels for napkins.

Use oilcloth fabric for tablecloths—it washes off with a sponge and you can cut the edge with scissors!

Use fabric—like this blue toile—for tablecloths. I use iron-on tape to make a hem.

Use table runners instead
of placemats.

Choose one color and follow through
with the flowers and glasses.

foolproof menus

Summer Dinner
Easy Gazpacho & Goat Cheese Croutons *64*
Hot Smoked Salmon *83*
Parmesan Fennel Gratin *176*
Crusty Basmati Rice *195*
Prunes in Armagnac *240*

French Dinner
Mussels with Saffron Mayonnaise *71*
Slow-Roasted Filet of Beef with Basil Parmesan Mayonnaise *122*
Provençal Cherry Tomato Gratin *173*
Green Beans Gremolata *169*
Perfect Pound Cake *208*

Birthday Dinner
Seared Scallops & Potato Celery Root Purée *146*
Balsamic Roasted Brussels Sprouts *196*
Carrot Cake with Ginger Mascarpone Frosting *213*

Thanksgiving
Thyme-Roasted Marcona Almonds *46*
Accidental Turkey *120*
Green Beans Gremolata *169*
Sweet Potato Purée *178*
Mushroom & Leek Bread Pudding *188*
Maple Pecan Pie *247*

Fireside Dinner
1770 House Meatloaf *129*
Orange-Braised Carrots & Parsnips *170*
Truffled Mashed Potatoes *187*
Stewed Rhubarb & Red Berries *235*

Family Dinner
Crispy Mustard-Roasted Chicken *119*
Crispy Roasted Kale *174*
Couscous with Peas & Mint *184*
Chocolate Cassis Cake *205*

Dinner for In-laws
Fresh Whiskey Sours *home 21*
Rack of Lamb *parties 172*
Orzo with Roasted Vegetables *parties 174*
French Apple Tart *basics 191*

New Year's Eve
Pomegranate Cosmopolitans *basics 41*
Filet of Beef with Gorgonzola Sauce *parties 82*
Herbed New Potatoes *paris 168*
Roasted Cherry Tomatoes *parties 85*
Baked Chocolate Pudding *basics 218*

Boss Comes to Dinner
Loin of Pork with Fennel *home 104*
Roasted Brussels Sprouts *tbcc 150*
Celery Root & Apple Purée *basics 169*
Pear, Apple & Cranberry Crisp *home 200*

---

tbcc	*The Barefoot Contessa Cookbook*
parties	*Barefoot Contessa Parties!*
fs	*Barefoot Contessa Family Style*
paris	*Barefoot in Paris*
home	*Barefoot Contessa at Home*
basics	*Barefoot Contessa Back to Basics*
easy	*Barefoot Contessa How Easy Is That?*

French Bistro
Kirs *paris 29*
Chicken with Forty Cloves
of Garlic *paris 113*
French String Beans *paris
160*
Couscous with Pine Nuts
home 101
Crème Brûlée *paris 222*

Snowy Day
Turkey Meatloaf *tbcc 138*
Roasted Carrots *tbcc 149*
Parmesan Smashed
Potatoes *tbcc 158*
Beatty's Chocolate Cake
home 165

July Fourth
Oven-Fried Chicken *fs 81*
Vegetable Coleslaw *tbcc 107*
Sagaponack Corn Pudding
fs 128
Peach & Raspberry Crisp
tbcc 190
Shortcakes *parties 146*

Quick & Elegant
Chicken with Goat Cheese
& Basil *home 114*
Roasted Carrots *tbcc 149*
Tagliarelle with Truffle
Butter *basics 152*
Panna Cotta with Balsamic
Strawberries *home 190*

Labor Day
Pink Grapefruit Margaritas
easy 37
Eli's Asian Salmon *home
118*
Tomato, Mozzarella & Basil
Salad *fs 64*
Sautéed Fresh Corn *parties
125*
Peach Raspberry
Shortcakes *parties 146*

Autumn Dinner
Real Margaritas *parties 134*
Indonesian Ginger Chicken
tbcc 125
Roasted Carrots *tbcc 149*
Herbed Basmati Rice *home
138*
Affogato Sundaes *basics 217*

Date Night
Juice of a Few Flowers
basics 37
Parmesan Chicken with
Arugula Salad *fs 82*
Stewed Berries with Ice
Cream *fs 148*

Father's Day
Fresh Peach Bellinis *home
237*
Steakhouse Steaks *easy 138*
Roasted Brussels Sprouts
tbcc 150
Baked Potatoes with Yogurt
& Sour Cream *basics 156*
Pear Clafouti *paris 186*

Valentine's Day
Lemon Chicken with
Croutons *paris 110*
Zucchini Gratin *paris 148*
Truffled Mashed Potatoes
187
Chocolate Mocha Icebox
Cake *easy 206*

sources

Unless otherwise noted, tableware and linens are privately owned.

Baccarat
800-215-1300
baccarat.com
Purple crystal glasses, page 263

Bloom
43 Madison Street
Sag Harbor, New York
631-725-5940
Tableware, pages 65, 81, 136, 168, and 262

H Groome
9 Main Street
Southampton, New York
631-204-0491
888-222-0552
hgroomeonline.com

Bergdorf Goodman
754 Fifth Avenue at 58th Street
New York, New York
212-872-8700
800-558-1855
bergdorfgoodman.com
Hotel silver serving pieces, pages 36 and 47

Ochre
462 Broome Street
New York, New York
212-414-4332
ochrestore.com
Tableware

index

recipe index